<u>the</u> mi**X**take <u>files</u>

A nit-picker's guide to
The X-Files

D1538138

by

Michael French

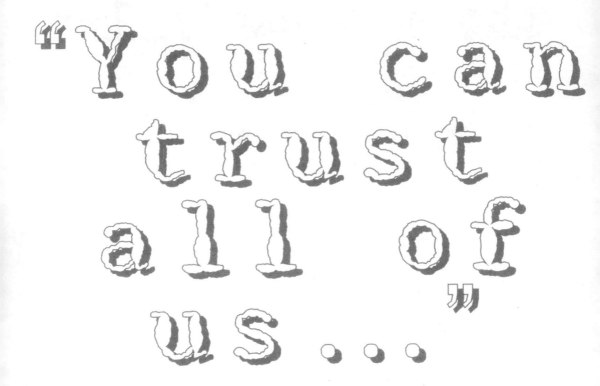

"You can trust all of us ..."

The Cigarette-Smoking Man
(a.k.a. Cancer Man)
3X16: "Apocrypha"

ACKNOWLEDGEMENTS

I first must thank the CompuServe X-Philes in the second Science Fiction Forum who all unintentionally contributed to this book in some way, as I lurked in the shadows taking notes. **Your craziness has not gone unnoticed :-)**

Chris Carter, Gillian Anderson and David Duchovny deserve a mention (along with the rest of the X-Files crew, past and present). To the people who got me (and millions of others) hooked after the first episode, thank you for such brilliant television.

Finally, but most importantly, thank you to my family and friends, who didn't seem to mind me re-watching episodes over and over and over...

INTRODUCTION

Welcome, fellow nit-pickers, to the ultimate nit-picker's guide to The X-Files. May I take this short moment to warn you that contrary to popular belief, nit-picking is not the petty criticism of minor details and it is, in fact, an art form. Yes, that way of noticing the "little things" is not to be frowned upon, and such words against the art are merely disinformation by the government, who are hoping that it does not become addictive.

This book is not designed as a criticism of the brilliant television show The X-Files, its crew, actors and anyone else involved in the process of making it. If there is any criticism, it is meant in a constructive way. The last thing I'd want is to upset the people who put together these great stories in a matter of days.

Okay, so far, the most innovative show on television has seventy-three episodes of non-stop quality under its belt and it's about time we started paying attention, real attention. It's time to get out the video collection of episodes one through seventy-three and watch those episodes for the scenes where Scully's hair is miraculously changed by unknown beings or when Mulder's computer goes missing, with nothing but a keyboard left to show it existed.

The nit-picks in this book follow a fairly basic pattern - they point out mistakes. Yes, I said mistakes. Although it is hard to believe that such an amazing show could be flawed, there is always the problem that little things can slip past the intelligent people that produce it and this is what this guide does (well it points out the mistakes, it doesn't create them). The nit's however, very rarely attack the basis of an episode, as all the plot lines in The X-Files always seem to fit together nicely. The nit's point out the humorous things, the bloopers and the great moments.

Each entry in this guide has at least five sections out of seven. The sections are the following: Episode Production Number and Title, Summary, and Episode Nit-Picks, followed by Recurring Actors, Best Line, Scenes, and Title Explanation. Some of these are self explanatory, some are not, so the descriptions below tell you what is in each.

Episode Production Number and Title

The production number is simply the record number designated by the production company, Ten Thirteen, to each particular episode. The first digit in the number corresponds to the season the episode originates from, the "X" tells the production company it is an episode of The X-Files, and the final number corresponds to the episode number of the particular season. An example is production number 3X22, which is episode number twenty-two from season three of The X-Files.

The episode title is the name designated to the episode by the writer, which refers to some aspect of the show. The titles themselves are unfortunately not given in the episodes' credits, and are also sometimes quite cryptic, hence the inclusion of the "Title Explanation" section (see below).

Episode Summary

The summary is a short description of what the episode is about, and is not a synopsis of the episode, for two reasons. Firstly, some fans may not have seen a particular episode or episodes so reading the brief description, which does not contain spoilers, will let them know as to whether or not they have seen the episode. If they haven't, they can choose to skip the nit-pick section of the entry. Secondly, some readers, including myself, find that complete synopses take up valuable book space and can always be found in another guide relating to The X-Files (not mentioning any names).

Episode Nit-picks

The nit-picks are the main point to this guide and vary in length for each particular episode, some having a long list of nit-picks, other having a short listing. The list itself is in full chronological order for that particular episode, so this can be used as an accompaniment to the particular episode.

The nit-picks themselves all point out various mistakes in the episode, be it in continuity, a plot discrepancy, or in the episode subject matter. The type of nit-pick is given at the end of each paragraph. As music has turned up quite frequently in the show I have included the Music Moment nit-pick also, which gives the name of a song that features in an episode and who performs it.

Recurring Actors

I don't know about you, but I have often watched an episode and wondered "Wasn't he/she that person from that other episode?" (It's never usually that vague, mind you.) It is a regular occurrence in The X-Files that actors are simply reused or recycled as different characters due to their skill and the fact that they live in Vancouver, meaning they can get to filming easier than other US-based actors. A lot of the time they have key roles or noticeable roles.

That is where this section comes in. Almost every entry has this section and contains a list of names which varies in number for each episode. At the back of this book, you will find the complete recurring actor listing which gives character names and episode titles, you can use this list to cross-reference with the names in each entry and find out what episodes the actor had appeared in previously.

Best Line

As the title suggests, this section gives the best line out of an entire episode, sometimes two are given, or a passage of dialogue is shown. The lines are either funny and/or very well known sayings from the show.

Scenes

This section can contain three types of scene reference. The first are scenes that may have been eventually cut from the episode (usually seen in the scripts but not in the final edit), the second are the most memorable scenes from the episode, and the third is any 'out-take' or 'blooper' that may have occurred during filming of the episode. This section may contain all, one, or none of these types of scene reference.

Title Explanation

As mentioned previously, some of the episode titles are very cryptic and require explanation. All entries have a brief sentence or two at the end of each to explain the meaning of the title.

Also, throughout this guide you will see various pages devoted to certain aspects of the show that fans would love emphasised or discussed. There are a few scattered around, focusing on various elements of the show.

So, the truth is not here in these pages, but some good fun is...

ALIEN TALLY BOARD

Extra-terrestrials are the first thing associated with The X-Files, but has anyone actually stood back to look at the show itself and realised how many types we've seen in the show? The list is huge! Not only are there very different types, but the series also suggests that there are hybrids of these life-forms.

It seems so far that there are at least seven types visiting or inhabiting various areas of this planet, so don't you think the Earth is getting pretty crowded now?

It's quite a list, so I've put each type into similar categories.

Don't you think the Earth is getting pretty crowded now?

LIST OF EXTRA-TERRESTRIALS

1. Shape-Shifters: Seen on various occasions in the show, most notably the Bounty Hunter sent to destroy the clone colonies **["Colony"**, **"End Game"**, and **"Talitha Cumi"**], and Jeremiah Smith **["Talitha Cumi"**]. It's also suggested that these aliens have the ability to heal wounds. If they're so powerful, why haven't they wiped out all the other species of alien in the course of universal domination? (And I don't think these are peace loving…)
Of course, we mustn't forget the sex-changing group from **"GenderBender"**, who also (sort of) come under this category.

2. Greys: This is the standard and common alien type, but they aren't as important as the Shape-shifters - which bleed that dangerous green blood - if you ask me. We've seen them in **"The Erlenmeyer Flask"** (fetus form), **"Little Green Men"**, **"Duane Barry"**, **"Anasazi"**, **"Nisei"** and **"731"**. You must remember though, that it is suggested that the bodies seen from **"Anasazi"** onwards are hybrids of the human/grey variety or are not even aliens at all and are covert government project side-effects.

3. Infestations: well it seems that any type of lower extra-terrestrial life form, not displaying any higher intelligence, is on this planet. So far we've had killer worms that may have been carried here by a meteor (did they pilot it to Earth?) as seen in **"Ice"**. There are the killer cockroaches, identified in **"War of the Coprophages"**. And there's also the spores from **"Firewalker"**, although the origin of the spores is not fully explained, could be alien, could have an earth-based origin.

4. Oil Based: We can't forget the slippery body snatching life-form which leaves that oily black liquid everywhere, from **"Piper Maru"** and **"Apocrypha"**.

5. Then there's the **radioactive** ones from **"Fallen Angel"**.
6. There are the **ghostly spirits** from **"Space"**.

7. And finally the aliens that apparently abducted Samantha Mulder and set up clone colonies on this planet (although they may be shape-shifters).

Season One

"The X-Files: Pilot"

A forensics medicine expert for the FBI, Doctor and Special Agent Dana Scully, is assigned to work with Special Agent Fox "Spooky" Mulder to debunk and analyze his work on the FBI's "X-files". Their first case deals with abductions of some kind in a group of high school friends, and as a small-town conspiracy is exposed, an even larger one, in the government, continues unknown to Scully and Mulder.

X When Scully first enters Mulder's office, the camera pans across the room, showing us what is pinned to the wall, and we see that he has a poster on the wall which reads, "I Want To Believe" and depicts a photo from a UFO sighting. Initially we are able to see the poster in its entirety. The shot then cuts to Scully, the poster is still visible behind her, but this time the bottom of the poster is partly obscured by a stack of papers.

Continuity

X This nit-pick comes from the very first question Mulder asks Scully: "Do you believe in the existence of extra-terrestrials?" By definition extra-terrestrial means something that is not of this planet and therefore alien. Scully replies by saying, "Logically, I would have to say no." It seems, so far, that Scully is talking about a disbelief in life other than that on our planet, but she goes on by saying "Given the distances needed to travel from the far reaches of space, the energy requirements would exceed a spacecraft's capabilities." It seems that Scully misunderstood the question, Mulder did not ask if she believed in UFO's or extra-terrestrials actually visiting this planet.

Continuity

Recurring Actors: Doug Abrahams, J.B. Bivens, Lesley Exen, Kata Gardener, Stephen E. Miller, Rick Reid, Malcolm Stewart

Best Line: This episode is one of the greatest examples of the differences in belief between Mulder and Scully:

> Scully: "Time just can't disappear, it's a universal invariant!"
> Mulder: "Not in this zip-code!"

Scenes: I have been told that the episode was originally supposed to start with a scene with Scully being requested, by the Cigarette-Smoking Man, to speak with the FBI superiors. My guess for its disappearance is that starting the episode with the viewer not knowing what was taking place, with Scully just entering the FBI building and keeping the viewer guessing, was considered to make a more interesting episode by Chris Carter and/or the production staff. The episode was also set to include a boyfriend for Scully, but the idea was cut at the last moment.

Title Explanation: This episode's name was originally **"The X-Files"**, but when it was granted a season of episodes, it was re-named **"Pilot"** as it was the pilot episode to the series.

Do you believe in extra-terrestrials?

"Deep Throat"

The bizarre behaviour and disappearance of an Air Force test pilot leads Mulder and Scully to Ellens Air Force Base in Idaho, where Mulder believes UFO experimentation with US test craft is taking place. However, Mulder is warned by an unknown figure that this case should be avoided at all costs...

At one point in the episode, Mulder and Scully witness a UFO flying in a way that would be impossible for normal aircraft. Shortly before this, the craft flying overhead flies at such a speed that it causes their car's rear window to smash into the car. After seeing the UFO, and having spoken with Emil and Zoë (the kids Mulder and Scully found sneaking out of the air base), Mulder and Scully are driving the same car but the rear window is now miraculously fixed.
Continuity

Later in the episode, Mulder and Scully are confronted by Men In Black who destroy Mulder's evidence and photos of the UFO's and search the other files Scully and he have. They also take away Scully's gun and remove the magazine from it. You can see that there are no bullets in the magazine, because you can see through a large gap in the middle. Being an FBI agent, wouldn't she be expected to have some ammunition in her gun at all times in case of emergency? And where did all the bullets go anyway?
Continuity

When Scully and Mulder are run off the road, there is a quick external shot (before Scully turns to see the car behind them) that shows what is supposed to be them being jolted as the car comes to a halt. The figures in the car are obviously not Gillian Anderson or David Duchovny, but are

stunt men, one of whom is wearing a very bad (not to mention big) wig.
Continuity

X Why is it that whenever a UFO appears in The X-Files, it is suddenly night-time? As the action flicked between Scully and Mulder at the Air Base, the time of day changed, night-time for Mulder, day-time for Scully. Did Scully spend the whole night waiting around in her motel room, and then get all worked up over his disappearance? (Obviously not, after the missing scenes reported below.)
Continuity

Recurring Actors: Andrew Johnston, Michael Puttonen, Gabrielle Rose

Best Line: "You didn't come to raid my mini-bar did you?"- Mulder has a one-liner for every occasion. Also: "Do you think if maybe we ignore him, he'll go away?"- one of Mulder's suggestions as an imposing Man in Black stands outside the car.

Scene: This episode originally contained quite a few scenes and lines that were eventually cut from the final episode. The most notable scenes were Scully at the FBI research library encountering Section Chief Blevins who classes Mulder's work on the X-files a waste of Bureau time and money. The other scene is where Scully, frantic to find Mulder, and without a car, runs to find Emil and Zoë to see if they have seen Mulder.

Title Explanation: The episode is named after the informant encountered by Mulder in this episode, and although he is not named in the episode, the script classes him as Deep Throat (during his final appearance). The name is taken from the Watergate scandal.

"Squeeze"

A friend of Scully's asks for help from her and Mulder on a case of some bizarre deaths. All these deaths have no obvious point of entry, no witnesses, and each victim has had their liver removed. During the uneasy help he gives, Mulder manages to find links to this case and other X-files which date all the way back to 1903.

X If Eugene Tooms was able to stretch his body to unimaginable lengths, why didn't he squeeze his way out of the handcuffs and escape when he was arrested?
Plot Discrepancy

Recurring Actors: Gary Hetherington, Kevin McNulty

Best Line: "Do you think I'm 'spooky'?" - Mulder to Scully after the insults from Colton and co.

Scenes: Initially, Mulder was supposed to have thrown a trash-can through the window to get inside Scully's house, but it was changed as she is supposed to live on a high floor (apartment number 35), so he just came in through the door.

Title Explanation: Eugene Tooms was able to stretch his body to extraordinary lengths, and fit through small spaces, but still found many a squeeze(!).

"Conduit"

Mulder drags Scully into a case where a young girl was abducted during a camping trip. Evidence from the girl's brother and mother indicates UFO involvement, and as Mulder and Scully try to find the girl, Scully believes that Mulder is paralleling this case with that of his sister's abduction.

✗ If Samantha Mulder was abducted twenty-one years ago, it would set this episode on August 24th 1994, that's during Scully's abduction.
Continuity

✗ It is impossible to gain such a large amount of information from such a small amount of binary code as Kevin wrote out. And Mulder only took a few pages of the code Kevin was writing, so how they managed to decipher a sonnet, satellite transmission or any one of those other items mentioned from that small amount of data is anyone's guess.
Subject Matter

✗ When Ruby is found, Scully says she is alive - but unconscious - and begins to give her CPR! The girl was alive, fine, she would probably regain consciousness later, no point choking her, as giving CPR to a living person would.
Subject Matter

Recurring Actors: Joel Palmer, Don Thompson

Best Line: "C'mon!... How could an eight-year old boy who can barely multiply be a threat to national security?... And people call me paranoid." Mulder to the government agents who class Kevin as a national security risk.

Title Explanation: The name refers to Kevin, the young boy in this episode who acted as a conduit for the messages being transmitted through television sets.

1X04

"Jersey Devil"

Mulder believes he has found evidence of the mythical "Jersey Devil" after a body is found half eaten in an area of the New Jersey forest, a case very similar to one dating back from the 1950's. While he encounters some harsh treatment from the local police department, Scully attends her godson's birthday party and ends up "getting a life" by going on a date with someone she meets there.

X The Jersey Devil was very good at keeping itself hidden, secret and unspotted for fifty years, otherwise there would have been many sightings of it. If that was the case, how did Mulder manage to catch a glimpse after spending only a night looking for it?
Plot Discrepancy

Recurring Actors: Bill Dow, David Lewis, Hrothgar Matthews

Best Line: I personally don't rate this episode very highly but there is some great Mulder and Scully interaction with some great lines, especially their closing passage:

Mulder: "Don't you have a life, Scully?"
Scully: "Keep that up, Mulder, and I'll hurt you like that beast woman."
Mulder: "30 million years out of Africa..."
Scully: "...And look who's holding the door."

20

And Mulder's very apt: "What's eating that guy?"

Scenes: Like many of the other episodes, this one was blatantly left open for a sequel, this time with the closing scene of a junior beast.

Title Explanation: The Jersey Devil is a real-life legend about a beast/creature that allegedly lives in the New Jersey Forest.

X Why were all the license plates on the cars in this episode covered up? The plates are never covered up in previous or subsequent episodes.
Continuity

1X05

"Shadows"

Mulder and Scully are mysteriously requested by unknown government agents to look at the two bodies of men who have had their throats crushed - from the inside. After Mulder uses a unique method to identify the bodies, he and Scully follow clues to a lady who seems to be surrounded by some powerful force...

X Mulder's method of gaining fingerprints from the corpses - by using his eyeglasses to take the prints - was very ingenious. Unfortunately, most of the shots in the early scene with Mulder, Scully and the "mysterious agents" included Mulder, and there is never enough time for Mulder to gain the prints, as we always see him doing something else.
Continuity

X This episode was set two weeks after Robert Graves' death, which was on October 3rd 1993, but Lauren Kyte's attack, which eventually involved

Scully and Mulder with the case, was said to have occurred on September 22nd.

Continuity

X The researchers who reported on Graves' death were obviously not as accurate as they thought, reporting his middle name as Thomas when his gravestone tells us it is Patrick.

Continuity

X When Mulder looses control and power of the car, it speeds backwards down the road and crashes into an approaching car and we are treated to an external shot of Mulder and Scully's car. Again, it is obvious that the occupants are not Gillian Anderson or David Duchovny, but stunt substitutes. Also, when the scene cuts back to the interior of the car, Mulder is looking at Scully, but in the exterior shot, the stuntman was looking at the driver of the car they have hit, which is the opposite to Scully's position.

Continuity

X So, Scully couldn't get into the room, due to the paranormal force? Well she would have if she had opened the door properly, by pushing it forwards, not pulling it towards herself, as she evidently did.

Plot Discrepancy

Recurring Actors: Lorena Gale, Deryl Hayes, Tom Heaton, Janie Woods-Morris

Best Line: "Do you know how hard it is to fake your own death? Only one man has pulled it off... Elvis" - Mulder to Scully on the subject of hoaxing death.

Scenes: I don't think this is as bad as Glen Morgan and James Wong (the writers) rate it, the most memorable scene has to be the finale in the office with the mini-hurricane. (Sure, it was just a wind-machine and a stack of paper, but I liked it.)

Title Explanation: A shadow is a little-used term for a ghost, and ghosts were the main subject of this episode.

1X06

"Ghost in the Machine"

Mulder's old partner asks for help with a case involving the strange electrocution of a company chairman. Deep Throat tells Mulder of a secret the company's building holds, raising questions as to whether or not a computer exists which can think for itself.

𝕏 After finding out Scully's phone number, the Eurisko computer dials her house, and while she is doing other things, accesses her computer (downloading "WILCZEK.DOC"). But somehow her computer is switched on after her modem answers the call; a computer has to be switched on physically: this cannot be done by a phone signal. Which is another problem in this episode - not that many people have their modem on auto-answer, like Scully has, so why did she set it like that? (Although Scully may have programmed her computer to say, "Mulder, where are you?" as that is all she seems to ask when they talk on the phone.)
Plot Discrepancy

𝕏 When Scully is investigating the voice on the phone line made to Drake before he was killed, she manages to piece together the voice as that of the computer systems programmer, Brad Wilczek. She does this by piecing together words from Wilczek's seminar recordings from digital audio tape (DAT). At one point we hear her skim through the tape and can hear the noise on the tape as if it was at high speed. Unfortunately, DATs, as Scully was using, do not make this sound when rewound or fast-forwarded while playing.

Subject Matter

X Eurisko accesses Scully's computer again later in the episode, when she is in bed, and the audience finds that the file WILCZEK.DOC is being read again. Why did Eurisko do this? Was there any reason for it to read the file again? Did it get bored?

Continuity

X Also, why did the phone ring when Eurisko called up the second time, and not ring when it called up the first time? Surely it should have rung both times, to signify that someone was calling? (It was just a plot device to alert Scully to what was going on the second time, but is made all the more unbelievable with all the plot holes and errors it throws up.)

Continuity and Plot Discrepancy

X And there is another nit-pick as Scully manages to make a call while her phone line is already busy. She should either have found that the phone was engaged when she tried to make a call (because Eurisko was taking up the line) or disconnected the line as she broke the connection. So, if this was to be taken realistically, Scully would never have been able to trace the call, and the episode would have probably ended in disaster.

Plot Discrepancy

X When Mulder's ex-partner goes to the building, the computer system notices he is in the elevator, and in order to preserve itself, causes the lift to fall to the ground. We see a shot of Lamana inside the elevator, which is falling, and he is lying on the floor. If the elevator was falling to the ground, and at such a high speed to kill him, he should have stuck to the ceiling of the elevator, not the floor.

Plot Discrepancy

Recurring Actors: Gillian Barber, Marc Bauer, Tom Butler

Best Line: "I'm NOT a pain in the ass?" - Mulder.

Title Explanation: The Ghost in the Machine in this instance is the mind or intelligence the computer system seems to have. Arthur Koestler wrote a book of the same name.

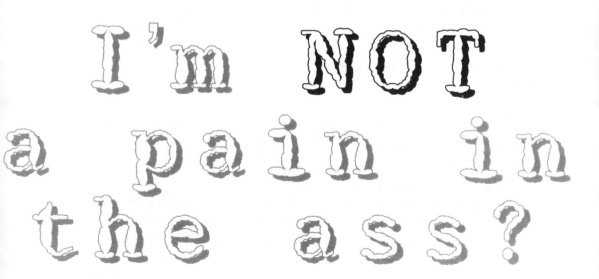

"Ice"

A strange transmission from the Arctic Ice Core takes Mulder and Scully, along with some scientists, to Alaska. The research team at the base have all been killed, apparently by each other. A sense of claustrophobia grows as it appears that there could be a murderer among Scully, Mulder, and the rest of the investigating team.

✗ There are slight differences between the version of the transmission made by Richter and the one which is viewed by Mulder and Scully, the differences are mostly longer or shorter gaps between sentences, most notably when Richter says, "It all stops, right here, right now" and the tape plays it with a gap in the dialogue that wasn't there before.
Continuity

✗ Scully finds that the worms have the desire to attack each other, by seeing two worms, in small containers, each acting strangely when placed near each other. The question is, where did the second living worm come from? They only had one that was alive.
Continuity

✗ When Scully, Hodge and Doctor DaSilva find that re-infecting a person kills off both parasites, they successfully try the procedure on the dog. Soon after, they say that the dog passed the worms in its stools. There are two problems with this: firstly, the worms were in the neck, so how their dead bodies made their way to the excretion system is unexplainable (typical for this series) and secondly, the dog passed the worms a bit too fast. Even if the worms did find their way to the intestine, going through the bodily system and excreting them would have take a lot longer than an hour or less.

Subject Matter

X At the end of the episode, Hodge informs Mulder and Scully that the AICP base was torched by the military, and as he does so, makes all the motions that the whole area is very cold, by blowing into his hands to keep warm. But if it was so cold why don't we see their breaths? And if this was Alaska, where was the snow?

Continuity

Best Line: Scully values her life more than evidence, Mulder evidently does not:

Mulder: "It's still there, Scully, 200,000 years down in the ice."
Scully: "Leave it there."

Scenes: Not sure if there was an actual scene, but this one is very good, and very tense.

Title Explanation: Deep in the ice was where the worms were.

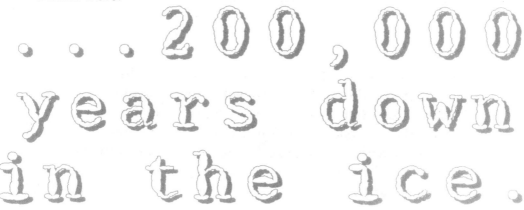

...200,000 years down in the ice.

"Space"

Mulder gets to meet a childhood idol - Lt. Col. Belt, a famed astronaut - when he and Scully are asked by a NASA scientist to investigate some strange cases of sabotage in space shuttle flights. Meanwhile, Belt is having strange visions, particularly one of the face from the well known "face on Mars" picture.

The first space shuttle flight was in 1981, but the type of space walk Belt took (which is only possible with a space shuttle) was claimed to have taken place in the mid 1970's as Mulder said he was fourteen when he watched it. Surely it should have been when Mulder was at least twenty?

Plot Discrepancy

Early in the episode, Michelle is in a car accident and is trapped in the overturned car. When we see her position in the overturned car, she is lying on her side but when Mulder pulls her out she is now lying on her back, suggesting that the accident caused her to be flipped upside down, but there isn't enough room in a car for that to happen. Also, Michelle is cut badly in the accident but the next day there is no evidence of the wound, which actually caused a lot of bleeding, suggesting it would still be visible.

Continuity

When Michelle tells Mulder and Scully that Belt has collapsed, they follow her, with Scully leading Mulder. But when they enter the office, Scully is now last. Being a medical doctor, I doubt Scully would let anyone go ahead of her as she should want to get to a patient as soon as possible.

Continuity

X When they find Belt under the table, everyone forgets that Scully is a doctor, with Mulder calling for a doctor and Scully doing nothing to help. Scully's lack of help is then contradicted when she gives instructions to the paramedics and even informs Mulder of the possibilities of Belt having an aneurysm.

Continuity

X Belt eventually puts an end to his suffering by throwing himself out of the window, effectively putting an end to his life. Wouldn't hospital windows on very high floors be designed so that you can't jump out of them?

Plot Discrepancy

Recurring Actors: Alf Humphreys

Best Line: Three great Mulder/Scully exchanges:

Mulder: "You never wanted to be an astronaut when you grew up, Scully?"
Scully: "Guess I missed that phase."

And:

Mulder: (After meeting Belt) "I have to admit, I've fulfilled one of my boyhood fantasies."
Scully: "Yeah, it ranks right up there with getting a pony and learning to braid my own hair."

And:

Scully: "Evidence of what?"
Mulder: "Alien civilisations."
Scully: "Oh, of course!"

Title Explanation: The whole episode is about space travel, and what happened to an astronaut while in space.

1X09

"Fallen Angel"

Deep throat informs Mulder of the government's attempts to clean up and cover up a crashed UFO site. Mulder quickly arrives with no time to lose, but is soon caught by the army and imprisoned over night. While at prison he is not the only person interested in the UFO, as he encounters a man who knows a bit more about Scully and Mulder than you might expect.

X There is a time error when the teaser of the episode is compared with the scenes after the main titles. Initially we are told that the UFO was first found at 12:57 A.M. on Day One and the military is alerted, Deep Throat then tells Mulder of the UFO and says he has at least 24 hours. We see that Mulder is at the town by night-time, but we are again told that it is 12:57 A.M. on Day One. It should either be a different time, or a different day.
Continuity

X As Mulder gets Max a glass of water, we see Max tuck his hair behind his right ear (which is plot device so we will later see Max's scar when he lies down) and we see him push the hair off of his shoulder away so it hangs behind him, but when Max drinks the water, his hair is still tucked behind his ear, but now back on his shoulder.
Continuity

30

✘ When Max lies down after his seizure, Mulder notices a V-shaped scar behind Max's right ear, but when he sees Scully, he tells her it is behind his left ear. Not only that, but the photos Mulder shows Scully have the scars behind the left ear also.
Continuity

✘ Fifth and sixth degree burns, eh? Well wouldn't that mean charred to pieces? The record only goes up to fourth degree burns, which is when the body is burnt down to the bone.
Plot Discrepancy

Recurring Actors: William MacDonald, Michael Rogers, Alvin Sanders

Best Line: The final exchange between Mulder and Scully as he goes to see the FBI board:

Scully: "Good luck."
Mulder: (with crutches after his encounter) "I'll break a leg."

Scenes: The nit-pick regarding burn types has its own funny out-take, with Scully running to some burnt bodies and shouting to Mulder, *They're done!*

Title Explanation: A "Fallen Angel" was the term given by the military unit in this episode to specify a crashed UFO. Also, a "fallen angel" is another term for a ghost, meaning a spirit that had fallen from the sky, just like the UFO in the episode.

"Eve"

Mulder and Scully investigate a murder case where two people were killed in an identical fashion, at the exact same time, but in different ends of the US. When it turns out that both victims have daughters who are identical, they begin to uncover a government project that involves tampering with cloning and genetics...

X The episode begins with a chilling start, a man being found dead, murdered as Mulder later explains by exsanguination (which is to die instantly by having the blood removed from the body, in this case, having the jugular in his neck pierced). The man's daughter, Teena, and two neighbours find him dead outside, sitting in a garden swing. If the jugular was pierced, it is expected that almost all of the blood in the body would have sprayed out of the small hole like a high-pressure jet of water, as blood pressure in that particular blood vessel is very high. If that was the case, where had the blood gone when Teena's father was found dead? There is an answer, as Scully later explains, that there was rain shortly after the first murder, which would have caused the blood to drain away. If it did rain, why wasn't the body or the surrounding area wet then when it was found?

Continuity

X As the story progresses, Mulder and Scully visit one of the clones, Eve 6, at a prison. She explains that she has extra chromosomes of the normal chromosome sets. Unfortunately, this theory is a bit inaccurate as extra chromosomes cause havoc in the bodily system during pregnancy and the foetus would be aborted by the body immediately. This is not, however, the only scenario that could be encountered with extra chromosomes, retardation and Downs Syndrome are also other known effects. You would not gain heightened strength, intelligence, or any of the other powers claimed by Eve 6 through extra chromosomes.

Subject Matter

X When Sally Kendrick has kidnapped the girls, they sit eating, drinking and talking in the motel room. They are all drinking from paper take-away cups. However, after the girls have disposed of Eve 7, Mulder looks at the cup and it has turned into glass. It was obviously changed during shooting so the green residue from the digitalis was easier to see on camera, but the whole scene suddenly loses credibility and continuity.

Continuity

X The end of the episode gives us a slight twist - the remaining Eve, number 8, arrives at the prison. Firstly, unlike Mulder and Scully, she was not given a flashlight or warned about Eve 6. Secondly, it seems strange that nobody realises that the visitor looks identical to the older prisoner. Of course, we were told that no one had had a good look at her (which in itself seems quite odd as Eve 6 had been institutionalised for quite some time), but when Mulder and Scully went to see Eve 6 she could easily be recognised as being similar to Sally Kendrick as all the older Eve's do. Also, it took the connections of Deep Throat to get Mulder and Scully, two FBI agents, into the prison, so how did Eve 8 get inside with just a letter? Through the backdoor perhaps, like in **"Paper Clip"**?

Plot Discrepancy

Recurring Actors: Garry Davey, Maria Herrera, Robert Lewis, Tasha Simms, Gordon Tipple, George Touliatos

"Best Line: Mulder really likes his UFO terminology:

> Mulder: "Abducted."
> Scully: "Kidnapped."
> Mulder: "Pot-ay-toe, pot-ah-toe."

Title Explanation: The Eves were the female products of the Litchfield Experiments, the males were called Adam. The first male and female on the earth are known as Adam and Eve, as taken from the Bible, and the Eves were the first of the race to have such heightened powers.

1X11

"Fire"

An old "flame" of Mulder's, Phoebe Green, who he met while in England and who works for Scotland Yard, asks for his assistance to help her protect a visiting Parliament member who may be under attack from a pyromaniac serial killer. Not only does this seem to make Scully jealous but re-lights the lost love Mulder once held for Phoebe.

X Really more of an observation, but this is the episode where what is now known as the "X-Files Office" made its first appearance. Gone are the early days of season one where Mulder or Scully's office would change repeatedly episode after episode. The question is: if this is Mulder and Scully's office (she's spent a lot of time in there in this episode, I doubt she'd sit in Mulder's chair to feel big), why isn't her name on the door in this or subsequent episodes?

Continuity and Office Irregularity

X There's a nice piece of stock footage thrown in here, when Scully types at her computer, stolen straight from **"Squeeze"**. How can you tell? Same camera movements, and the photos on the desk are the same (presumably from the Tooms case).

Continuity

X Here could be the reason Scully makes mistakes about dates and times. At one point in the episode, Scully looks at her watch, and we see it is one where there is both an analogue and digital display. When she looks at the watch, the digital display reads 4:22:10, but the analogue hands read 5:05.

Continuity

X If you watch when Mulder gets out of his car before he goes in the house, to find Phoebe and the MP kissing, he is wearing his trenchcoat, when he bursts in through the door he is wearing only his jacket. You can see how the editor has tried to cover up the boo-boo by showing the viewer as little of Mulder as possible, making it a very quick flaw.

Continuity

X Again, more burn problems! Cecil apparently has fifth and sixth degree burns, and as we all now know (from **"Fallen Angel"**) - shall we all say it together? - the burns rating only goes up to four!

Plot Discrepancy

Recurring Actors: Lynda Boyd, Alan Robertson

Best Line: Even though this set was cut from the script, I still find it interesting as it sort of stretches past the platonic nature of the Mulder and Scully relationship, and still retains some of the show's dark humour:

> Scully: "Never let it be said that you wouldn't walk through fire for a woman, Mulder"
> Mulder: "And never let it be said that I wouldn't do it for you again, Scully."

Also:

> Mulder: "Well, that's one of the luxuries to hunting down aliens and genetic mutants. You rarely get to press charges."

Title Explanation: Quite obvious seeing as this one is about a pyromaniac, but it also covers Mulder's fear of fire, and the fact that Mulder classes Phoebe as fire.

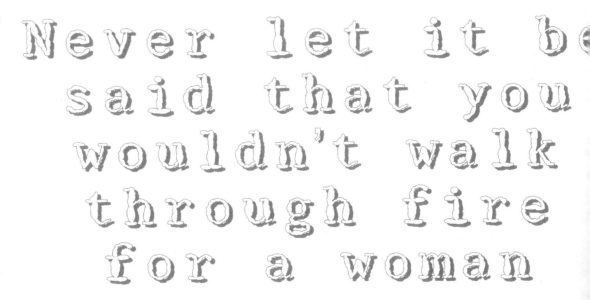

Never let it be
said that you
wouldn't walk
through fire
for a woman

"Beyond the Sea"

Scully is faced with emotional turmoil when her father dies, and she sees a vision of him shortly after his death. She stops herself from researching an X-file on psychic phenomena, and she and Mulder travel to see Luther Boggs, a man previously convicted by Mulder and awaiting execution on Death Row. Boggs claims that he is now psychic and will help solve a kidnapping if his death sentence is dropped. The tables are turned as Scully, who Boggs tells can send her father a message, becomes the believer and Mulder is the sceptic of the claims.

X Watch carefully when Scully is driving home from the prison and notices the signs that Boggs described. As she looks from the angel statue and the "waterfall", it can be clearly seen that various shots have been mirrored as the parting in her hair changes sides of the screen along with the lights of the car behind her and the rear view mirror.
Continuity

Recurring Actors: Fred Henderson, Don MacKay

Best Line: "Last time you were that engrossed it turned out you were reading the Adult Video News." Despite the tragedy, Scully can still hold banter with Mulder.

Scenes: This is definitely one of the stronger episodes of the season, with a stunning performance by Gillian Anderson. (Real award fodder.)

Title Explanation: "Beyond the Sea" was the song playing at William Scully's funeral and later sung (very badly!) by Boggs.

"GenderBender"

A set of sexually related deaths, which do not tell if the killer is male or female, initially puzzles Mulder and Scully, they find a connection to the killings, and subsequently, The Kindred, a community which distances itself from civilization for a particular reason...

X The Kindred have distanced themselves so much from society that they've gone insane! As Mulder and Scully enter their settlement, you can see they are hanging their laundry, and chopping wood, in the rain!
Continuity

X When Mulder and Scully are asked to leave the Kindred settlement for a second time (when Mulder has rescued Scully from doing the "wild thing" with Brother Andrew) Mulder initially has his arm around Scully, but leads her away by the hand, and when the camera cuts to a different angle, he has his arm around her again.
Continuity

Recurring Actors: Doug Abrahams, Paul Batten, Lesley Exen, Michelle Goodger, Mitchell Kosterman, Nicholas Lea, Kate Twa

"Best Line: There are quite a few funny one-liners in this episode, here are a few of the best:

> Scully: "So what IS our profile of the killer? Indeterminate height, weight, sex; unarmed, but extremely attractive?"

> Scully: "There's something up there, Mulder."

Mulder: "Oooh, I've been saying that for years."
Mulder: (While commenting on The Kindred) "The Addams Family finds religion."

Scenes: The X-Files out-takes contains a longer version of Mulder's radar love speech in the X-files office, saying things like "the ultimate nookie magnet … Spanish fly incarnate!" There is also an out-take from when Mulder questions the store owners on The Kindred - the male says "They usually shop down there at the feed-store… there they go" before the Kindred's horse and cart drives by, causing Mulder to point at him and say "You're clairvoyant!"

Title Explanation: The Kindred were the gender benders, being able to spontaneously change sex.

1X14

"Lazarus"

An old friend of Scully's, Jack Willis, is shot when a bank-robbing suspect is caught in a trap. Scully, who is helping Willis with the case, shoots the suspect in turn, and both men are sent to hospital, with Willis being the survivor. When Willis seems to have gone through a transition, it appears that life saving was not all that went on in the Emergency Room.

X Mulder claims that they are unable to track the kidnappers as they are using Scully's cellular phone, but we know this is untrue as the Cigarette-Smoking Man managed to trace Mulder to a desert in **"Anasazi"**. Secret government technology or not, surely they would be able to roughly find the area the call was being made from by tracking its signal?
Plot Discrepancy

𝕏 When Willis is practising at the firing range, we can see that he has already fired eight shots into the target. We then see him fire another five which would suggest that he has made thirteen holes in the target, but when we see the target, there are still only eight holes. He must be losing his touch to miss a target directly in front of him five times... **Continuity**

Recurring Actors: Jay Brazeau, Peter Kelamis, Callum Keith Rennie, Mark Saunders

❝Best Line: "That's a nice story." Mulder's well placed one-liner manages to lighten the atmosphere after Doctor Varnes tells the agents how a near death experience changed a man's attitude so badly that he "strangled his wife with an extension cord."

And Mulder's FBI peers make no attempt to hide their mockery of Mulder:

FBI Agent #1: "OK, everyone grab a seat and pay attention. Mulder says he's got something."
FBI Agent #2: "What? An alien virus or new information on the Kennedy Assassination?"❞

Title Explanation: Lazarus was a character brought back to life by Jesus Christ in the Bible, the name itself has been used on other occasions in a story of resurrection or of a similar vein. In this instance it refers to Willis' being brought back to life, but being possessed by Dupre.

"Young at Heart"

A man convicted by Mulder in one of his early cases, John Barnett, seems to return from the dead years later, threatening to kill Mulder and his friends. While Mulder has to find out if Barnett is still alive or if a very good copy-cat is on the loose, Scully finds links between a doctor who has had his licence revoked and Barnett's apparent death.

X When Perdue is killed by the young Barnett in his home, watch the way he falls to the side of the bed. When the camera angle changes, you can see that the body has moved.
Continuity

X Scully should be worried after John Barnett accesses her answer-phone, but not because she is being watched; someone is pretending to be her mother! (The voice on the answer-phone is not that of Sheila Larkin, the actress who played Mrs Scully in **"Beyond the Sea"** and other episodes in the second and third series.)
Continuity

X The scene with Barnett holding the cello player hostage flicks between shots of Mulder walking forward and Barnett shouting at Mulder. We see Mulder's ear-piece all the way up until he fires his gun, when the ear-piece is gone, Mulder's hair has also changed slightly here so these are obviously parts of different takes or shooting sessions spliced together.
Continuity

Recurring Actors: Robin Mossley, Gordon Tipple

41

"Best Line: Mulder's exchanges with other women aren't as successful:

    Agent Henderson (Graphologist): (while looking at
      Barnett's handwriting) "This guy a friend of yours?"
      Mulder: "Yeah. I play golf with him every Sunday…
      what do you think [of the handwriting]?"
        Agent Henderson: "You just brought this in ten min-
        utes ago!"
        Mulder: "You're slipping, Henderson."
        Agent Henderson: "Ten minutes may be enough time
        for you, Mulder. 'Course I wouldn't know that from
        personal experience."

    And later in the same scene:

    Mulder: "Thanks, Henderson. I owe you one."
    Agent Henderson: "Promises, promises."

    Title Explanation: Dr Ridley had performed experiments which prevented or reversed the ageing process and had been carried out on John Barnett, making him younger, so now Barnett was young at heart. This itself raises a nit-pick, because Barnett wasn't actually "young at heart", he may have wanted to be young and had the appearance of being young, but he was originally old.

The truth is out there…, but so are lies.

"EBE"

A UFO is shot down near a US Army Base, and a truck driver loses control of his vehicle when he sees a UFO. Both cases seem unrelated until Deep Throat steps in to help Mulder and Scully, bringing with him lies as well as truths.

✘ At one point, Mulder and Scully lie in wait of the approaching truck and as it goes past they pull away to follow it. When they do, a reflection of the camera filming the scene can be clearly seen in the car's rear passenger window.
Continuity

✘ Scully and Mulder are following the truck when they encounter a bright light, which initially seems to be a UFO encounter. After the flash of light, the truck is now without driver and has been turned around. We later learn that the encounter was a set-up, so the reversal of the truck cannot be blamed on alien activity (although I doubt they visit Earth to just to turn trucks around), so who turned the truck around?
Plot Discrepancy

✘ When Mulder and Scully climb into the truck, Scully waits as Mulder gets in, holding his flashlight for him; when Mulder reaches out to pull Scully up, she is no longer carrying it. It is obviously a splicing together of different takes, because when Scully and Mulder take readings to check if there really was a UFO encounter, Scully is again holding the flashlight and standing in the exact same position as before she climbed into the truck.
Continuity

Recurring Actors: Allan Lysell

Best Line: The very first Lone Gunmen appearances were fun, and Scully's line about truths and lies is all too true in the X-Files universe – "The truth is out there, Mulder, but so are lies."

Title Explanation: An EBE was the subject of the episode, meaning Extra-terrestrial Biological Entity, which Mulder and Scully were trying to track down.

1X17

"Miracle Man"

After an attempt at healing from faith healer Samuel Hartley, a lady dies, but not from the serious condition she already suffered from. Mulder and Scully are called in after another death to investigate the murder claims against Samuel Hartley and his Miracle Ministry.

X So Scully was taught about miracles in medical school? What did they say: "… And if you cannot revive the patient, hope like hell they'll live!"?

Recurring Actors: Lisa Ann Beley, Chilton Crane, Campbell Lane

Best Line: "No wait. This is the part where they bring out Elvis." Mulder's religious beliefs still remain sceptical at the faith healing drive. Also, this exchange from the same scene:

> Mulder: "I think I saw some of these same people at Woodstock."

Scully: "Mulder, you weren't at Woodstock."
Mulder: "I saw the movie!"

Title Explanation: The miracle man is Samuel who apparently had the power to heal people.

1X18

"Shapes"

Scully and Mulder are thrown into a boundary war between the residents of an Indian Reservation and some ranchers when they investigate a murder, apparently caused by a wolf-like creature.

✗ Ish describes his own encounter with a Manitou and he claims that the eyes remained human. Yet, when Lyle changes to the beast a short while later, his eyes are one of the first changes noticeable and they are not human.
Continuity

✗ And we're supposed to believe that Scully couldn't hear Lyle from inside the bathroom, and vice versa? Yeah right… I suppose that noise must have been the radio, along with those fangs being calcium deposits, yes, Dr Scully?
Continuity

✗ While Lyle is changing into the beast, we see that he rips the shower curtain with his right hand, indicating that his nails have grown to claw-like lengths, but when the shot changes, his hands do not have claws or long nails.
Continuity

Recurring Actors: Dwight McFee, Paul McLean, Renea Morriseau

Best Line: Mulder really doesn't like his "Spooky" nickname:

> Ish: "You should be Running Fox... or Sneaky Fox."
> Mulder: "Just as long as it's not Spooky Fox."

And I'm only including this, not as it is a memorable line, but because it is the most outlandish SRE (Scully Rational Explanation) ever - Scully classing the fangs on Lyle as "calcium deposits".

Scenes: A well known missing scene shows Mulder and Scully's progress in their car being blocked by a cow, and with Scully shouting "Baseball glove... leather purse!" at it to scare it away. Before that however, there is a short exchange which also failed to make the cut:

> (The Agents are trying to decide how to get around the problem)
> Scully: "Have you ever had any dealings with a cow?"
> Mulder: "Agent Scully, WHAT are you implying?"

Title Explanation: Werewolves are, in essence, shape-shifters (this is the only way I could find that "shape" would fit into the episode's story).

You should be Running Fox... or Sneaky Fox.

"Darkness Falls"

Mulder and Scully go in search of a group of missing loggers in Washington State. It seems the loggers have cut into something thousands of years old, and have suffered the consequences. Mulder and Scully are left alone in the forest with the Park Ranger, trying to avoid the same consequences.

X There is a continuity error when Mulder, Scully and the Park Ranger are looking at the growth rings of the trees. When Mulder first gets to the tree, there is a large crack in it. When the camera closes in on the rings, the crack is not there.

Continuity

X Mulder and Scully find a cocoon high up in a tree in the forest which contains a dead body ("barely" a male), which is one of the loggers. But no one seems to ask how the cocoon arrived up there or why the logger was up there. The only logical explanation is that the logger climbed the tree himself, and was cocooned while up there, but why? Surely he can't have been trying to escape the insects, as they could fly. And I doubt the entire hoard of insects - dangerous or not - could pick him up and put him there.

Plot Discrepancy

X It is suggested in the episode that the insects do not like light, which is why, when darkness falls, that the insects come out to kill. Mulder, Scully and everyone else in the cabin seems to forget that lighting a fire would ward off the insects when the power to light the bulb ran out.

Continuity

Recurring Actors: None

Best Line: "Anything strange, unexplainable, unlikely, boyfriend" - Mulder's reply after being asked by Scully "But what am I looking for?" concerning the missing loggers.

Title Explanation: When darkness falls the insects would come out, as they could not stand the light.

1X20

"Tooms"

Eugene Tooms, who has now been institutionalised for eight months, is set free after no evidence that he was responsible for the four recent killings can be found and when Mulder's claims that Tooms was the killer in the murders from 1903, '33, and '63 are dismissed. Scully is warned by Assistant Director Skinner of the FBI that all their cases must be "by the book" if the X-files are to remain open, while Mulder tracks Tooms and attempts to stop him gaining his fifth and final liver.

✘ Eugene Tooms was in the institute for eight months, and when he is released, his original place of residence has now been demolished and a shopping mall has been built in its place. Isn't eight months a bit too fast for that type of structure to be built? And who gave the builders the right to knock down the place anyway? Okay, Tooms was in care while it was destroyed, but he still has rights - it is his home.
Continuity

✘ When Mulder manages to escape Tooms from his nest under the escalator and switches it on, the now active escalator pulls Tooms away and kills

him. To pull Tooms away the escalator must have been travelling down, but when we see the blood on the steps, it is travelling up.
Continuity

Recurring Actors: Andre Daniels, Glynis Davies, Frank C. Turner, Timothy Webber

Best Line: "I'm sure." Spoken by Tooms after being told he would be able to "squeeze in" to the room he was residing in.

Scenes: Out-takes galore as Duchovny adds words to the script that don't belong. As he questions Tooms, who is ignoring Mulder while making his way into his van, he says, "I have a Norwegian elkhound... I use him to hunt moose... for my hair." And on another take of the same scene, Mulder asks Tooms, "Where can I get a jump-suit like that?"

Title Explanation: The title is the main culprit's, Eugene Tooms', last name.

Anything strange, unexplainable, unlikely, boyfriend.

"Born Again"

A little girl who may have witnessed the ghost of policeman Charlie Morris kill a living policeman, Detective Barbala, becomes the subject of an investigation. When it appears the girl has psychokinetic powers and was born when Morris died, Mulder suggests that she may not have seen the ghost of Morris but may be him.

X Didn't Mulder and Scully arrive at the scene of the murder a little too quickly? The detectives were still taking pictures of the scene. Even if they were just asked along by Detective Lazard, they still would have had to travel from DC to New York, quite some distance away (although if Scully was driving, they may have made it in time…)
Continuity

Recurring Actors: None

Best Line: "Mrs Bishop won't go for that. Not in this lifetime, anyway." Spoken by Scully after Mulder's claims of reincarnation.

Title Explanation: Being re-born, or born again was what happened to Charlie Morris. Only this time, he was re-born as Michelle Bishop.

Not in this lifetime...

"Roland"

Foul play is afoot among scientists at a research facility where a high speed engine is being designed. The suspect is a mentally retarded janitor, but how could he have operated the jet engine which killed the first scientist, and who has been successfully finishing the equations that help solve the engines' problems? Scully and Mulder investigate...

X During the teaser, we see that Roland has locked the first scientist in the wind tunnel and has activated the motor. The doctor panics and decides to run to the end of the tunnel. Obviously he is trying to get as far away as possible, but if the motor was as powerful as we are later told, how did he manage to hold on to the grating for so long before being sucked in? And why didn't he duck down in the corner next to the motor, which would have kept him safe? Surely the scientist who helped design the motor would know not to stand in the air current as he would most definitely be killed?
Plot Discrepancy

X Scully and Mulder visit the laboratory where Grable's head is being frozen, and Scully asks a scientist if she can read Grable's file, which he promptly delivers from a row in the room. Now, in the interests of security, wouldn't these personal and confidential files be kept elsewhere, like an office, not in a tray in a lab?
Plot Discrepancy

X Nolette uses a chewing-gum wrapper to cover his own keycard's magnetic strip so he can access the cryogenics laboratory, but this surely cannot be true. That type of lock requires a magnetic strip to read, and placing a piece of silver foil over an invalid strip would not affect the lock or trick it into thinking that it was the required key.

Subject Matter

X Also, after entering the lab, Nolette seems to know the access code to decrease the temperature in the freezing tanks. Where did he get the codes? (Although it was probably in the loose files left lying around in the lab.)

Plot Discrepancy

Recurring Actors: Garry Davey, Sue Mathew, Kerry Sandomirsky

Best Line: The opening lines do prove that Scully does do other things than autopsies and write FBI reports, and gives a quick laugh too:

Mulder: "How was the wedding?"
Scully: "You mean the part where the groom passed out or when the dog bit the drummer?"

Mulder: (after seeing the "accident" with the nitrogen) "I don't think they'll be doing this experiment on Beekman's World."

Title Explanation: Roland was the mentally retarded janitor in the episode.

. . . when the dog bit the drummer?

"The Erlenmeyer Flask"

Deep Throat calls Mulder and tells him to watch a TV news report on a man being chased by the police. At first, this is all the information he gives Mulder, but later he ends up helping Mulder and Scully, help which has dire consequences for all involved...

X If you watch the chase of the fugitive doctor during the teaser carefully, you will notice that when he looks into the rear view mirror, he speeds past a sign that reads "Vancouver Dry-dock Company Ltd.", but this episode was set in Washington DC. Obviously, the production crew overlooked this sign, which gives away the location where the scene was filmed.
Continuity

X When Scully, the medical genius, is on the phone to Mulder at the genetics laboratory, she makes a slip-up. She tells Mulder that chloroplasts are plant cells, when they are, in fact, only small parts of plant cells.
Subject Matter

X Towards the end of this episode, Scully comes face to face with what appears to be the foetus of an extra-terrestrial. Why didn't she take any sort of sample from the foetus as evidence? Mulder and her have always said how they need proof, and she had seen what was in this "original tissue" and how valuable it was to the government, or group, that killed the genetics doctor (and that was no regular car accident). (And are we to believe that they'd just let her walk away with the thing...? After all the security guarding it?)
Plot Discrepancy

Recurring Actors: Ken Kramer, John Payne

Best Line: "Okay, Mulder, but I'm warning you, if this is monkey pee, you're on your own" - Scully to Mulder after he asks her to try and find out what the brown substance in the medical flask is. Funnily enough, when the scene with that line in was shot, as Scully leaves the room, Mulder quips, "It's an acquired taste."

Deep Throat's dying words also are important here as they spawned one of the show's mottoes: "Trust No One."

Scenes: If you ask me, it's Mark Snow's stirring accompanying music that adds to the tension the episode builds up, especially when Scully obtains the "original tissue" from the facility.

Title Explanation: The Erlenmeyer flask in this instance is the medical flask found in Doctor Berube's laboratory that was labelled and contained the substance of "Purity Control".

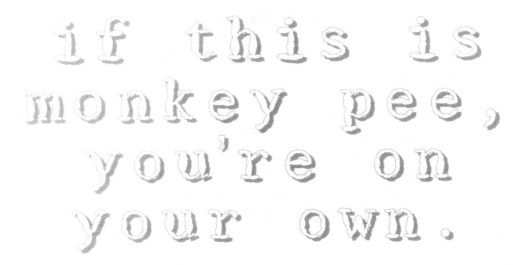
if this is monkey pee, you're on your own.

SEASON ONE: FAMILY SCORECARD

DANA SCULLY: During the first year Scully unfortunately lost her father [William], and received heavy amounts of emotional turmoil afterwards. Her mother [Margaret] made a quick appearance, but her sister [Melissa] and brothers [Charles and William/Bill Jr.] failed to show up, but there were some other red-heads at the funeral for William Scully - could this have been them?

FOX MULDER: As mysterious as their own son, Mr and Mrs Mulder made this season a no-show, but we did learn of Mulder's only sibling: Samantha. Taken from their home by an unknown force at the age of eight (he was twelve) she is the reason for his quest into the unknown - he will find her - or so he thinks.

JEOPARDY!

You ever wondered how many times Mulder and Scully's lives have been placed in jeopardy by the "monster of the week" or the latest conspiracy? Here's the current standing:

Number of times Scully has been in jeopardy alone: 16

They are: An attack by Eugene Tooms in **"Squeeze"**, a breath of fresh air in **"Ghost in the Machine"** and kidnapping by her "friend" Jack Willis in **"Lazarus"**. A not-so-random shooting in **"Young at Heart"**, an encounter with a werewolf in **"Shapes"**, and abduction by persons unknown starting in the episode **"Duane Barry"**. Sat on the brink of death in **"One Breath"**, almost infected with deadly spores in **"Firewalker"**, was abducted again, by Donnie Pfaster in **"Irresistible"**. A voodoo curse tried to stretch its hands all the way around her neck in **"Fresh Bones"**, and she came face-to-face with a shape-shifter and was abducted again in **"End Game"**. Was tossed around like a rag-doll in **"The Calusari"**, and was almost infected with a disease in **"F.Emsaculata"**. Then there was the time she was abducted by the cannibalist group in **"Our Town"**, came face-to-face with a fat-sucker in **"2shy"**, and was brain-washed into thinking that Mulder was against her in **"Wetwired"**. (By the way; number of times Scully has been abducted: 5 - she should renew her personal insurance if you ask me.)

Number of times Mulder has been in jeopardy alone: 15

They are: Mind-wiping by the government in **"Deep Throat"**, an attack from a beast woman in **"Jersey Devil"**, and near-infection with an alien parasite in **"Ice"**. He confronted his fear of fire in **"Fire"**, was shot in **"Beyond the Sea"**, and was stuck under an escalator with the stretchy-mutant **"Tooms"**. He was then kidnapped by the Crew Cut Man in **"The Erlenmeyer Flask"**, was stuck in a bathroom with the taps on in **"Excelsius Dei"**, and then fought a shape-shifter in **"End Game"**. Was nearly blown to pieces in the buried box-car in **"Anasazi"** and was almost killed by The Puppet in **"Clyde Bruckman's Final Repose"**. Back to the box-car - he was almost blown up again in **"731"**, and ka-boomed in **"War of the Coprophages"**. He then became possessed in **"Grotesque"** and was stuck with rat-boy-turned-alien Krycek in **"Apocrypha"**. (Number of times Mulder has wound up in hospital: 5.)

Number of Times Mulder and Scully have been in jeopardy together: 7

Trapped with prehistoric bugs in **"Darkness Falls"**, kidnapped by Satanists in **"Die Hands Die Verletzt"**, and aged drastically in **"Dod Kalm"**. They then turned renegade against the government in **"Paper Clip"**, were both almost shot in **"Pusher"** with a deadly game of Russian roulette, and were stuck with a hoard of killer cats in **"Teso dos Bichos"**. And finally, they were trapped on a rock in **"Quagmire"**.

Number of times David Duchovny has been on "Jeopardy!": once, and he lost to Stephen King.

Season Two

"Little Green Men"

Mulder and Scully, who have now been separated with the X-Files division shut down, are assigned to different areas of the FBI. Scully is back teaching forensic medicine at the FBI academy, and Mulder has been assigned to surveillance and wiretaps. Mulder is given a location by his Congress connection, Senator Matheson, where evidence of alien contact may be kept. He is soon chased as he heads to Puerto Rico, putting his life in jeopardy.

X Probably the most major of the nit-picks, mostly due to the fact that this episode disagrees with Mulder's initial claims of his sister's abduction in the first episode, **"Pilot"**. In this episode, we see a flash-back, and Mulder is at home as a boy, playing a game of "Stratego" with his sister in the living room; they are not, as he claimed previously, in their bedroom. However, as Mulder said, the event may not have even happened so the details have become jumbled up, but we know that his sister was abducted, in some way, so this is still inaccurate.
Continuity

X The Senator is a very clever man, managing to write while looking the other way...
Continuity

X At one point Scully is trying to access Mulder's computer, to find out where he has gone, and has to guess his password to try and find out where he has gone. After a few guesses she correctly finds it is "TRUSTNO1", which has eight characters in it. Scully typed nine keys into the computer before pressing "ENTER", what was the ninth for?
Continuity

✘ When Scully is caught in Mulder's apartment she claims that she feeds his fish for him while he is away. The only problem is, Mulder's fish-tank is empty; which shows just how good those surveillance agents were, like when they mistook a sheet of paper which had "Galactic Latitude" written on it for a printer's test page.
Continuity

✘ Why was Scully wearing a trench coat in Miami, somewhere known for its warm climate, when everyone else (even the agents following her) were wearing summer clothes? Obviously because Gillian Anderson was pregnant at the time, but they could have used a body double and close-up facial shots as they did for some of the scenes in the other early season two episodes.
Continuity

✘ Unlike the way the episode portrays it, the Radio Telescope at Arecibo in Puerto Rico is not redundant and shut down, and it was not just used for the SETI project, it still runs many other projects.
Subject Matter

✘ Mulder had to climb the fence surrounding the Radio Telescope's control room to get inside, so how did Scully manage to get a truck past the gate, waiting outside for their getaway?
Plot Discrepancy

Recurring Actors: Lisa Ann Beley, Cecere Fulvio, Deryl Hayes, Gary Hetherington, Dwight McFee, Bob Wilde

Best Line: "That would be bad for the fish." Spoken by Scully to one of the surveillance agents who find her in Mulder's apartment and tell her to dump the spilt fish food in the tank. Ironically, there are no fish.

Title Explanation: During a covert meeting with Scully, Mulder explains that he may have been seeing or imagining "little green men" all his life, causing him to follow his crusade for the unknown. He paralleled his case with that of George E. Hale, who had the Palamar Observatory built because an elf told him how to fund the project.

2X02

"The Host"

A dead body is found in the Newark sewer system, and Mulder is given the case. He believes it is just a routine murder, but after a warning from an unknown figure - who says solving the case is imperative to the reinstatement of the X-files - and Scully's autopsy of the body, it seems that there is more to the sewers than meets the eye.

X I find it quite unlikely that the Flukeman would be considered a being with rights, to be tried or punished under the justice system. I mean, the thing was a freak of nature, wasn't human, and the government is the first to cover up any other type of life-form (after **"Ice"**, **"Fallen Angel"** etc.) so why do they take it to be institutionalised?
Plot Discrepancy

Recurring Actors: Marc Bauer, William MacDonald, Don MacKay, Hrothgar Matthews, Gabrielle Rose, Ron Sauve

Best Line: The scenes with Mulder and Scully, though very short in the beginning of this season, do get some great banter:

> Mulder: "This isn't where you tell me some terrible story about sushi is it?"
> Scully: "Maybe you'd rather hear what you can catch from a nice rare steak...?"
> Mulder: "So... what, the murder weapon was a top sirloin?"

Title Explanation: The flukeworm required a host to survive.

"Blood"

Mulder is asked to investigate a sudden spate of mass killings in a town which previously hadn't had a single murder in living memory. His investigation turns up broken electronic displays at all crime scenes, along with a strange organic substance, so Mulder turns to the Lone Gunmen for help.

X If you watch carefully when Mulder looks at the clipboard in the murdered mechanic's workshop you will notice that he is wearing surgical gloves as not to disturb the crime scene. But when the camera cuts to him running his finger down the list on the clipboard, he is no longer wearing gloves. Mistake with the hand double. Not only is it an error, but a very obvious one seeing as he cracks the "Pardon my rubber" line after looking at the clipboard.
Continuity

X There is a slight flaw concerning the date on the banner at the blood drive. It reads September

30th, which would be during Scully's abduction.

Continuity

Recurring Actors: Andre Daniels, David Fredericks, George Touliatos

Best Line: By this point in the series, Scully expects Mulder to tie UFO pheonomena into every case:

Mulder: "There have been reported abductee-paranoia in UFO mass abduction cases."
Scully: "I was wondering when you'd get to that."

Title Explanation: The main person affected by the sprayings was Edward Funsch, who had a fear of seeing blood. This fear caused his abnormal behaviour.

2X04

"Sleepless"

A scientist is dead, his body having suffered as if he had been exposed to fire but there is no evidence of flames at the scene of death. Mulder is tipped off about the case by X, and begins to investigate a government project involving sleep deprivation. Along the way, Mulder is assigned a new partner, Alex Krycek.

X During the scene when Scully is instructing her class, we see her students taking notes, but at one point, when the camera pans to show us a near point of view for one of the students, the student's notebook pages are blank. Maybe her previous "spooky" behaviour while instructing her class **["Little Green Men"]** caused this student to be very cautious of Scully's words and teaching.

Continuity

Recurring Actors: Mitchell Kosterman, Nicholas Lea, Michael Puttonen, Don Thompson

"Best Line: This episode saw the introduction of Krycek, Mulder's assigned "partner" who eventually appears to be not what he seemed by the end of the episode. Now I don't know about you, but am I the only one who found the giveaway that Krycek wasn't so nice after his conversation with Mulder (below)? A nit-pick in itself really as we were always told to believe that all the FBI peers had classed him "spooky", so it would seem quite weird for one of them to be a Mulder supporter. And even then, wouldn't it be even weirder (and somewhat too good to be true) for such a supporter to be partnered with Mulder? Anyway, the passage below is not only their conversation but includes some Mulder-sarcasm as well:

Krycek: "I don't like being ditched like someone's bad date."
Mulder: "Sorry if I hurt your feelings."
Krycek: "Where do you get off copping this attitude? I mean... you don't know the first thing about me!"
Mulder: "Exactly."
Krycek: "You know, back at the academy some of the guys used to make fun of you..."
Mulder: "Oh stop it, or you're gonna hurt my feelings!"

Title Explanation: The title refers to the fact that the sleep deprivation project had caused those experimented on not to sleep for a long time.

"Duane Barry"

Mulder is requested to help at a hostage negotiation with Duane Barry a man who claims to have been abducted by aliens and wishes to return to his abduction site. Mulder encounters some scepticism from the rest of the negotiation team as Scully meanwhile finds that Barry may not be what he seems.

X There is a slight problem with the bar-code on the implant as something only microns across would not register with a checkout scanner due to its size, and the bar-code would have no effect on the scanner unless it was the code for an item of shopping, those things are very specific, and even have trouble when scanning normal codes.
Subject Matter

Also, while talking about the implant, wouldn't Scully recognise it (or at least be suspicious of it) after the **"Pilot"** episode?
Continuity

Recurring Actors: Tim Dixon, Michael Dobson, Fred Henderson, Nicholas Lea, Robert Lewis, David McKay, Stephen E. Miller, Frank C. Turner

Best Line: Agent Kazdin seemed to figure that the only thing Krycek was good for is being a servant:

Krycek: "Is there anything I can do?"
Kazdin: "Yeah... what's your name again?"
Krycek: "Krycek."
Kazdin: "Krycek... have you got your notepad?"
(Krycek gets out notepad)

Kazdin: "Grande. Two percent cappuccino with vanilla...
Agent Rich?"

Scenes: The X-Files has had some very good and edge-of-the-seat cliffhangers, and the final scene, with Scully screaming to Mulder's answer phone for help as she is abducted by Duane Barry, is still one of the best for shock-impact.

Title Explanation: The name of this episode is taken from the main culprit and suspect in the episode, Duane Barry. (Note: it was originally intended to be Duane Gary, but the name was already taken by a real FBI Agent.)

2X06

"Ascension"

Mulder resumes the chase for Duane Barry and his new hostage, Dana Scully, to Barry's original abduction site, despite Skinner's warnings that he is to keep clear of this case. Whether Mulder finds Scully or not, it seems that not everyone working with Mulder is what they seem.

X That increasingly haunting song that plays as Duane makes his getaway is "Red Right Hand" by Nick Cave and the Bad Seeds.
Music Moment

X Would the new cables on the cable car really be that unsafe for one passenger? Even if it was travelling at speeds over the limit?
Plot Discrepancy

X There is another problem with the time of day when the "UFO" (looks more like a helicopter search-beam if you ask me) arrives to take Scully away. It's early evening at one point, and then it changes to pitch-black darkness.

Continuity

Recurring Actors: Meredith Bain-Woodward, Peter LaCroix, Nicholas Lea, Steve Makaj, Bobby L. Stewart

Best Line: "Oh I don't know, maybe it's because I find it hard to trust anyone" - Mulder's reply when asked why he is so paranoid.

Scenes: As Duane Barry's dead body is revealed, Krycek, Skinner and Mulder make the three monkey signs of "Hear no evil, speak no evil, see no evil" in an out-take.

Title Explanation: The title could be named after a few things; it could be the fact that Mulder realised where Duane Barry was taking Scully with the tape recorded line of "ascend to the stars" which was the slogan for the Skyland mountain lift, or it could be the fact that Scully had ascended to the sky and was essentially in ascension as she was taken away by the aliens, government, or whatever.

I find it hard to trust anyone

"3"

Mulder begins work on the newly opened X-files, minus Scully. He begins tracking the Trinity murderers, a set of vampire fetishists, and ends up getting more than a little involved...

X Early in the episode we see that the murderers have scrawled an alleged passage from the Bible on a wall and Mulder claims it is John 52:54. John 52:54 doesn't exist in the Bible. What Mulder quotes is John 6:54.

Subject Matter

Recurring Actors: Roger Allford, Ken Kramer, Tom McBeath, Malcolm Stewart

Best Line: "How do you define normal?" - Mulder to Kristen Killar. (Good point!)

Title Explanation: The three are the Trinity murderers, who called themselves The Father, The Son and The Unholy Spirit. Also, it may just be a coincidence, but Scully was missing for three months.

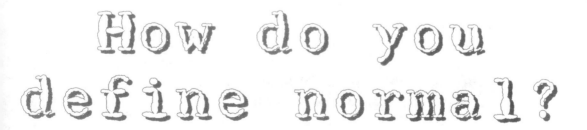

How do you define normal?

"One Breath"

Scully arrives at hospital comatose, delivered by persons unknown. As Mulder tries to find out what has happened to her, and whether she will regain consciousness, he faces many twists and turns in the government system.

X This episode is set in November 1994 (as per previous and following episode), yet Scully's medical chart contradicts this as it claims the events surround January 3rd 1994. I doubt the hospital would have been that prepared for Scully's sudden arrival, that they have the chart ready before she is abducted!
Continuity

X Byers says he has downloaded Scully's information to The Thinker, which is wrong. If you were downloading, it would be to yourself, not to someone else. To send a file to someone else on the Internet, or just from computer to computer, you would upload the information.
Subject matter

X If the Lone Gunmen were able to identify the branched DNA, why couldn't the doctors at the hospital do the same? Of course, the Lone Gunman are government watchdogs who know more secrets than you'd think but this is a woman in critical condition.
Plot Discrepancy

X Was it wise of Mulder to shout "Hey!" at the man who had stolen the vial of blood? Good FBI tactic. Why not just sneak up on him?
Plot Discrepancy

X If you watch Mulder's front door carefully when Melissa goes to see him, you'll notice the number "2" off of his door number of "42" has fallen off. (There is a reference to the missing number in The X-Files novel number 3, "Ground Zero".)

Continuity

Recurring Actors: Jay Brazeau, Lorena Gale

Best Line: Okay, so I'm only putting this one in because of this book, but it's still funny, and one of my fave's:

Langly: "You look down, Mulder. Why don't you come over Sunday night? We're all hopping on the Internet to discuss the scientific inaccuracies of Earth 2."
Mulder: "I'm doing my laundry."
(Note that Mulder never says this in the original script - obviously more of David Duchovny's improvising.)

Scenes: This episode's out-take is the famous "nipple-tweaker" when Fox Mulder takes a quick twist of a comatose Scully's nipples, causing her to sit up as if being defibrillated by medical equipment.

Title Explanation: Scully's father, who spoke to her in a vision while she lay dying, told her that life passed as if it was as short as "one breath".

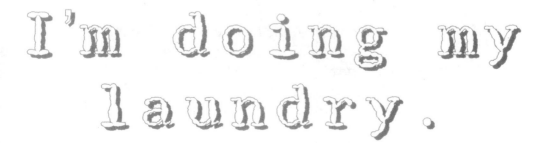

I'm doing my laundry.

"Firewalker"

Scully, now back at work on the X-files, travels to a federal research post in a volcano with Mulder to investigate the strange goings on with the equipment sent there. Mulder and Scully find the research team, minus a scientist, and it seems that a new silicon-based life-form has been unearthed and is slowly killing the team off...

X So, the case of **"3"** and **"One Breath"** both occurred in early November (lasting about ten days between the two) and this case commenced on November 11th? Scully sure recovered well didn't she? Should be called Super-Scully if she needed no rest at all after the complications caused by the branched DNA.
Continuity

X As the case progresses, we learn that the parasites needed a host, in this case the humans, to spread and survive. If that was the case, how did they survive for years in the volcano, which had no hosts?
Plot Discrepancy

X When Scully tests the parasite, she says she simulated the environment it would live in, and we see her heating a sample in a Bunsen burner, isn't that a little cold compared to the intense heat in a volcano?
Plot Discrepancy

X If the parasite grew into the large pole that burst out of the neck, wouldn't it choke you as it grew?
Plot Discrepancy

Recurring Actors: David Kaye, David Lewis

Best Line: Dead-pan all the way...

Scully: "What if he's already dead?"
Mulder: "He'll have a tough time answering my questions."

Title Explanation: The firewalker was the volcano probe that was damaged and led to Mulder and Scully being called in to investigate.

2X10

"Red Museum"

The bizarre treatment of school children, who are turning up with "He is one" or "She is one" written in marker-pen on their back takes Mulder and Scully to Wisconsin, where they encounter a vegetarian cult and some experimentation with links to "The Erlenmeyer Flask".

X There is a problem with the idea that the camcorder was filming through a hole in the glass. The hole was very small, and I doubt you would be able to see everything in the room we are told you can. And it could not have been a two-way mirror as when Mulder smashes the mirror, it has paint on the back.
Plot Discrepancy

Recurring Actors: Gillian Barber, Robert Clothier

Best Line: "Well, wherever he was coming from, I'd say that was one hell of a house call" - Mulder's words after seeing the plane crash.

Title Explanation: The Red Museum was the vegetarian cult featured in the episode.

"Excelsius Dei"

Scully brings in the case of a nurse who claims to have been raped by a supernatural force at a nursing home. Determined to solve the case, Scully finds evidence of drug abuse at the home while Mulder believes something has been unleashed, eventually encountering a force first-hand.

X At the beginning of the episode, when Mulder and Scully arrive at the Nursing Home, you can clearly see that the sign on the gate at the entrance says "Excelsis Dei", a title which disagrees with the episode's name.
Continuity

Recurring Actors: Tasha Simms

Best Line: Yet again, the writers find another way to hint at Mulder's porn habit:

Mulder: "Whatever tape you found in that VCR isn't mine."
Scully: "Good, because I put it back in the drawer with all the other tapes that aren't yours."

Title Explanation: "Excelsius Dei" is taken from the name of the nursing home in the episode, but note the difference in spelling mentioned above.

"Aubrey"

A police woman unearths the body of an FBI agent missing from 1942, and does not know how she found the burial site. Mulder and Scully step straight in, finding that it is not just appearance that can be inherited from your parents.

X During the beginning, Scully is reading a file in the office and turns pages over as she reads, yet when the camera cuts to Mulder's point-of-view - looking at Scully - the pages are no longer overturned.
Continuity

X The use of a cellular phone seems forgotten when Scully and Mulder find out that BJ may have inherited Cokely's tendency for murder. Instead of rushing to the house they could have just called her and told her to leave. Although, Mulder and Scully do use their phones a lot in the series, maybe the batteries had run down?
Plot Discrepancy

X When Mulder and Scully arrive at the house, we see that he is driving the car, Scully in the passenger seat. Mulder has to power-down the car, unbuckle his seat-belt, etc., yet he still manages to make it to the house before Scully, who only has to undo her seat-belt and hop out. And this happens many a time in the show, not just in this episode. (Unless she waited for him, and he is constantly rude and ungentlemanly towards her.)
Continuity

Recurring Actors: None

Best Line: There are quite a few good Scully and Mulder exchanges, so I'm throwing them all in:
(the pair stand looking at dental X-rays)
   Scully: "Any cavities?"
      Mulder: "I brush after every meal."

   Mulder: "Using psychology to solve a crime was something like... umm..."
      Scully: "... believing in the paranormal?"

      (Scully has a hunch about the reasons BJ knows about the murders)
      Mulder: "You mean a hunch?"
      Scully: "Yeah something like that."
      Mulder: "That's a pretty extreme hunch."
      Scully: "I seem to recall you having some pretty extreme hunches."
   Mulder: "I never have!"

Scenes: This one is almost unnoticeable because the viewer's attention is supposed to be on BJ as she digs up the body in the basement, but if you watch as Scully and Mulder come down the stairs, Scully trips, only to be caught by Mulder.

Title Explanation: Aubrey is the name of the town where the case takes place.

"Irresistible"

Scully and Mulder arrive in Minneapolis at the request of another agent to look at some desecrated graves. While Mulder believes this isn't an X-file and simply the work of a death fetishist, Scully seems amazingly sickened by the case which seems to trigger some memories of her abduction.

X In the graveyard at the beginning of the episode, you can see Ray Soames' tombstone, from the **"Pilot"** episode.
Continuity

X During the autopsy, Scully says the date is November 14th, placing the case immediately after **"Firewalker"**. Slight problem: Mulder and her should still be in quarantine after the incident at the volcano and if this day is taken as the 14th then the case is overlapping with **"Firewalker"**. Did they escape the quarantine? And how did they fit in the other previous three cases? (Maybe the Chris Carter episodes occur in a parallel universe?)
Continuity

X I'm a little worried about our Miss Scully and her self-preservation techniques. I would have expected that by now that she would have learnt some form of self-defence, and I would suspect it to be compulsory being an FBI Agent. Here's the score; Scully in car, Scully being followed in car by Pfreaky Pfaster, Scully run off road by Pfaster (look out, here it comes), Scully allows Pfaster to whisk her away to his make-over with death? It is obvious that when the car has stopped she isn't unconscious, did she think "Oh great, what a perfect end to an otherwise emotionally distressing day, what could happen next? I'll wait here with my eyes closed to find out..." I would have though she would have been particularly wary of anyone and anything, or even produced her gun, especially given the mood she was in.

Plot Discrepancy

✗ When Scully pushes Pfaster back into the bath tub, his arm becomes wet, but in the next shot his arm is now dry.

Continuity

Recurring Actors: Glynis Davies, Kathleen Duborg, Dwight McFee, Mark Saunders, Denalda Williams

Best Line: "People videotape police beatings on darkened streets, they manage to spot Elvis in three cities across America everyday, but no one saw a pretty woman forced off the road in a rental car" - Mulder's speech after finding that Scully has gone missing.

Title Explanation: It's a bit of a mysterious title this one, but are we to expect anything else from Chris Carter? The name could mean that Donnie Pfaster found his fetish irresistible.

"Die Hands Die Verletzt"

A young boy has been killed, and evidence points to witchcraft. Scully dismisses the idea of Satan-worship, but her tone changes when it rains frogs. The local school seems to be the centre of trouble, with suicides, a strange Parent-Teacher committee ,and where no one seems to remember hiring the substitute teacher.

X The teaser tells us that one of the girls at the accidental summoning is called Kate, yet later on, that very same girl is called Shannon. The events of the teaser must have been so traumatic that she has undergone an identity crisis!
Continuity

X The python that ate Ausbury must have been very clever, seeing as it managed to get his hands out of the handcuffs. Not only that, pythons swallow its prey in one piece, meaning that it would have been unable to eat a whole human, let alone start eating from one leg first.
Subject Matter

Recurring Actors: Doug Abrahams, Michelle Goodger, P. Lynn Johnson, Larry Musser

Best Line: "Mulder! Toads just fell from the sky!" Even Scully's mind seems to have changed when the mentioned event takes place.

Scenes: From the out-takes; when Mulder drinks from the water fountain (and notices the spinning of the water), it squirts straight in his eye.

The out-takes tape also shows Mulder and Scully reading Morgan and Wong's final message to the characters a bit differently than aired ("It's been nice working with you"):

> Mulder: "It's been nice using you again on our own
> show."
> Scully: "F*ck off - the Wongs."

> **Title Explanation:** "Die hands die verletzt" is
> German for "the hand that hurts", and is spoken by
> the teachers during the teaser. The hand is meant to
> be Mrs Paddock, who is implementing the pain of evil.

2X15

"Fresh Bones"

Mulder and Scully are called in to investigate the death of a soldier who has driven himself into a tree, his wife suspecting a
voodoo curse. The other soldiers are all behaving strangely as
well, but their superiors are in full denial of the curse and any other
power.

X I've looked, I've looked again, and I've re-double-
looked, and there are no nit-picks at all in this episode.
Mr Gordon; give yourself a big clap (and what a good
episode as well).

Recurring Actors: Roger Cross, Kata Gardener,
Peter Kelamis, Callum Keith Rennie

> **" Best Line:** "I'll admit the power of suggestion
> was considerable, but this [voodoo prevention
> charm] is no more magic than a pair of fuzzy dice."
> Scully argues her sceptic viewpoint into the

ground (despite the fact that the said artefact later saves her life).

Scenes: An out-take shows Chester forgetting one of his lines in the burger bar with Mulder questioning him. When he does, Mulder demands answers from the boy and pretends to strangle him for not answering.

Title Explanation: Fresh bones were what those practising voodoo would pay more for, presumably because they were from the newly dead, as told by Chester Bonaparte.

2X16

"Colony" (Part one of two)

A set of people who are all identical are murdered and Mulder and Scully investigate unofficially. When they find another look-alike, before the killer does, they meet a CIA agent who claims to have the same interests as Mulder. As the case grows in complexity, Mulder receives a message from Skinner of a family emergency. When he arrives at his parents' house he come face to face with the cause of his obsession with extra-terrestrial phenomena.

X The teaser, while interesting, and for the first time on The X-Files telling a story in flashback, has a minor error. Mulder is wheeled in, in a very death-march style, and Scully rushes in soon after, arriving just on time to tell the doctors how to save him. We see that an oxygen mask has been put on Mulder, and as the shot changes to show Scully talking with one of the doctors, we see in the background that Mulder has no mask on. Then, when the shot changes again, the mask is back on.
Continuity

X Scully tries to make sure she isn't followed, so she jogs to a bus station and goes to a motel. Mistake number 1: making a phone call on a bus full of people. It is unlikely, but she still could have been followed. Mistake number 2: The Bounty Hunter was already on the bus, how did he know what bus Scully would get on?
Plot Discrepancy

X Mulder's answer-phone is heard to have two different opening messages in this episode, also differing from the one heard in **"Duane Barry"** and **"Ascension"**.
Continuity

X Scully's hair. I've tried very hard to keep clear of mentioning the constant changes in style of our redhead's hair during scenes but this one is too obvious to miss. When Scully encounters all the Gregors at their lab, we are treated with close-ups of Scully pointing her gun and the clones. As the shots flick from one to the other, Scully's hair changes positioning. At one point it is slightly messy with strands at the back of her head highlighted by the light, the next minute the strands are tucked away.
Continuity

X Okay, so Mulder's cellular phone was out of action because he was hit by the car (if you can't lose your gun...) and it prevented Scully from calling him. So why didn't he call her on her cellular?
Plot Discrepancy

Recurring Actors: Linden Banks, Tom Butler, Bonnie Hay, Andrew Johnston, Ken Roberts, Michael Rogers

Best Line: Mulder makes quite a leap in a near nit-pickable event which causes him to trust Ambrose Chapel:

Scully: "Whatever happened to trust no one, Mulder?"
Mulder: "I changed it to trust everyone. Didn't I tell you?"

Title Explanation: As "Samantha" tells Mulder, the aliens have established a colony on Earth and are cloning themselves.

2X17

"End Game" (Part two of two)

Mulder, with the help of Skinner and "Samantha", must bargain with the Bounty Hunter to save Scully, but the trap backfires and "Samantha" is missing again, and this time may be dead. Fortunately, clues lead Mulder to a group of identical women and other information sends him on a trek to the Arctic Circle.

X The poisonous fumes from a dying Gregor-clone killed the agent in Syracuse in the previous episode, yet when Scully sees the decomposing Samantha clone, there are fumes, and they have no effect on her.
Continuity

Recurring Actors: Colin Cunningham, Bonnie Hay, Andrew Johnston, Allan Lysell, Beatrice Zeilinger

Best Line: "Wonderful, I've never slept better" - Mr X to Mulder after being asked "How was the opera?"

Title Explanation: An endgame is a final sequence of moves in a chess game or any other game, and in the instance of this episode it is relating to the final sequence of events in the story, like the fight between Mr X and Skinner, and the confrontation between Mulder and the Bounty Hunter.

2X18

"Fearful Symmetry"

A zoo which has never had a successful animal birth is investigated by Mulder and Scully for the possibility of alien abduction of its animals. The case is mingled with other problems, as when WAO protesters battle against the zoo, and when the zoo is threatened with closure.

✗ What is Mulder babbling on about with "astrological" co-ordinates and variation? The term to use is astronomical co-ordinates, astrological would concern your star-sign. (Madame Selma sees an elephant entering Sagittarius...)
Subject Matter

✗ It seems tigers are the exception when it comes to teleportation. All the other animals that were taken were returned two miles away, south-west, except the tiger which was "beamed" back into its cage. Quite a coincidence as the WAO activist was in there at the same time.
Continuity

Recurring Actors: None

Best Line:

> Scully: "...an invisible elephant?"
> Mulder: "I saw David Copperfield make the Statue Of Liberty disappear once."

He then later says (after finding a piece of an old newspaper on the floor):

Mulder: "Ahh... local paper. I want to see if David Copperfield's in town."

Scenes: Out-takes again arrive with Mulder telling Scully and Willa of Sophie's final message to him, but David Duchovny acts it as a game of charades, the solution being a film, four words - "Gorillas in the Mist". Unfortunately, Willa has no idea what it meant.

Title Explanation: The title is taken from the poem "Tyger Tyger" by William Blake, specifically the line: "could frame thy fearful symmetry?"

2X19

"Dod Kalm"

Scully and Mulder's investigations lead them to Norway's equivalent of the Bermuda Triangle, after a washed-up warship captain and his crew are found days after disappearing but having aged what seems like decades.

X Mulder, who allegedly spent time in England studying, obviously didn't study his surroundings that much (or read the map that was standing in front of him). Leeds isn't even close to where he points on the map, it's further up and more mainland; therefore it wouldn't have any ports.
Subject Matter

X There is a very funny clip in the beginning of this episode, involving Scully's coat. She enters

Mulder's office and places her coat over the back of a chair. After she has had her conversation with Mulder about the missing boats, he goes to the chair and picks up Scully's coat to put it on! (I guess David Duchovny still hasn't dropped the ladies clothing habit from "Twin Peaks".) The scene then cuts back to Scully as she talks to Mulder and the camera turns to him. He is putting a coat on, but it isn't Scully's coat, that's back on the chair where she initially left it, he is now putting his coat on.
Continuity

✗ By the end of the episode, Mulder and Scully have both fallen victim to the increased ageing and now have the outward appearance of very old age. When they are rescued at the end of the episode, Scully awakes in hospital along with Mulder and the appearance of heavy ageing has almost disappeared. How did the doctors reverse the ageing and return both to normal?
Plot Discrepancy

Recurring Actors: Mar Andersons, Stephen Dimopoulos

Best Line: Desperate times call for desperate measures:

Scully: "I looked everywhere and this is all I could find. It's sardine juice, half dozen lemons, and uh… the water from a snow globe."
Mulder makes noises as if to say "Sounds good!"

And another of Mulder's fun-in-the-face-of-death lines:

Mulder: "I always thought when I got older I'd

maybe take a cruise somewhere… but this isn't exactly what I had in mind… the service on this ship is terrible, Scully."

Scenes: Anderson and Duchovny apparently were very put off by the endless make-up sessions they had to go through to look aged, and Anderson managed to fit it in during a very memorable out-take. Scully originally tells Mulder how she is so sure, after her out-of-body-experience, that there is nothing to fear in death, yet in the out-take, she tells him she is sure that "Howard Gordon is a dead man!"

Title Explanation: When translated from its Norwegian origin, "Dod Kalm" means "dead calm", referring to the state of the sea. (I don't think it is a coincidence that there is a film called "Dead Calm" which features a group of people stranded on a boat in the ocean.)

2X20

"Humbug"

The death of the "alligator man" and other similar murders takes Mulder and Scully to Gibsontown, a small town inhabited by side-show performers. While there they must find what is paranormal among the inhabitants and try to find the killer before more victims are claimed.

X The song playing on Hepcat Helm's radio is Screamin' Jay Hawkins singing "Frenzy".
Music Moment

X The brilliant scene with the cricket is flawed, unfortunately, as Scully takes the bug and goes to pop it in her mouth with her right hand. When she shows the uneaten bug to Mulder, it is in her left hand. Her uncle must have been a very good magician.

Continuity

Recurring Actors: Alex Diakun, John Payne, Gordon Tipple

Best Line: As if, in a Darin Morgan episode...? The best line, in all that fun?

Title Explanation: A reference to P.T. Barnum who thought up the term of "humbug". There's also the humbug of the episode, with the viewer being led to believe that the killer would be the Figi Mermaid, but eventually turns out to be Lanny's twin.

2X21

"The Calusari"

A Romanian family begins to suffer from some strange deaths. The first is of the family's youngest boy, and a photo which was taken shortly before his death seems to suggest some sort of supernatural intervention, pulling Mulder and Scully, and other strange forces, into the case.

During the opening scene, Charlie's father has two ice cream cones, one has one scoop of ice cream, the other has two. He goes to hand Charlie the cone with two scoops but when the camera cuts to Charlie's father's perspective, his father is handing him the cone with one scoop. It cuts back to Charlie's point of view and the father is now holding the one-scoop.

Continuity

Recurring Actors: Bill Dow, Campbell Lane, Joel Palmer

"Best Line: Scully's growing scepticism of a paranormal force is laced with sarcasm:

> Doctor Burks: "In 1979 I witnessed a guru named Sai Baba create an entire feast out of thin air."
> Scully: "Too bad you didn't take a picture. You could have run it through your computer and seen the entire Last Supper."

Title Explanation: The Calusari was the Romanian group summoned by the grandmother to force away the evil spirit of Michael Holvey.

2X22

"F. Emasculata"

Mulder and Scully are sent to a prison to help with the capture of some escaped fugitives, but when they arrive at the prison find men in Biohazard suits - not required for this actual type of operation - walking around. It soon becomes apparent that a deadly contagion has been let loose in the prison and the escapees are also infected...

X There is an obvious flaw in the continuity here, when Scully is in the furnace room for the second time. After talking with Mulder on the phone, she finds an insect in a pustule on one of the bodies. At this point she has a surgical mask hanging around her neck, and the camera cuts to a shot of the bug being extracted. When it cuts back to her, she is now miraculously wearing the mask properly, and she

cannot have placed it on with her spare hand as we earlier saw that two hands are needed to put the mask on.
Continuity

Recurring Actors: Lynda Boyd, Chilton Crane, Morris Paynch, Alvin Sanders, Angelo Vacco

Best Line: Here's a good one:

Scully: "According to the briefing, the prisoners escaped while hiding in a laundry cart."
Mulder: "I don't think the guards have been watching enough prison movies."

Title Explanation: F. Emasculata was the type of bug found in the pustules on the bodies. The "F" stands for Faciphaga.

2X23

"Soft Light"

A former pupil of Scully's asks for her and Mulder's help in a case of bizarre disappearances. The missing people all seem unrelated, and the only clue is a scorch mark in the floor of the area where they were last. Mulder and Scully soon become heavily involved with the case and find evidence of a physics project that has gone awry.

X In the teaser, there is a major flaw as to what Chester's shadow can actually do. It seems that the shadow is able to move under doors! I know my shadow can't do that, can yours?
Plot Discrepancy

X At one point in the story, Mulder and Scully are informed by Chester's colleague that his

shadow had been transformed into a black hole by "dark matter". The dark matter theory exists so there are no problems with that story, but if Chester's shadow was a black hole, why didn't it suck in or swallow any other material that it touched, other than the people who were killed? Surely Chester would have touched his own shadow? (It's hard not to!) So he would have been killed too.
Plot Discrepancy

✗ When Chester is confronted by the two policemen in the alley, he warns them not to approach him as he is dangerous. Unfortunately they pay no attention and, as they circle him, one of them steps into his shadow, and is sucked in. Everything is fine up until this point, and when Chester turns to see the burn marks of where the cop previously stood, his shadow should stay in place. Unfortunately, this doesn't happen and his shadow is now behind him again, killing the other cop. This shouldn't have happened as there was only one light source in the alley, causing only one shadow, not two.
Plot Discrepancy

✗ The first victim (Margaret Wysnecki) is not connected with Chester in any way other than the fact that she had been at the train station, so why was she killed in her home? It suggests that he was at her house, but the other people who had died had either worked on the project or came into contact with his shadow accidentally. There was no reason for Chester to be at her house.
Plot Discrepancy

✗ Why did Kelly Ryan's funeral service have a casket when she was reduced to almost-nothing by Chester's shadow?
Continuity

Recurring Actors: Forbes Angus, Steve Basic, Craig Brunanski, Guyle Frazier, Kevin McNulty, Kate Twa

Best Line: Even X manages to get in a one-liner;

> Mulder: "He believes the government is out to get him."
> X: "It's tax season… so do most Americans."

This episode also hints at the possibility of Tooms being the killer:

(Scully suggests the ventilation shaft being a possible path of escape)

> Ryan: "You don't think anyone could've squeezed in there?"
> Mulder: "You never know."

Title Explanation: Soft light, or diffused lighting, was the kind of light Chester Ray Banton had to be in to render his shadow unable to kill. Soft light does not cause shadows, so no shadow, no killing.

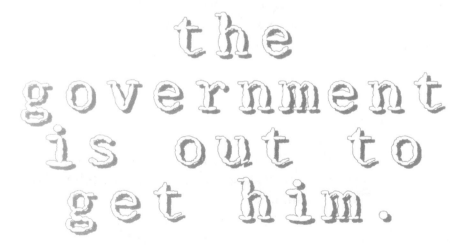

the government is out to get him.

"Our Town"

The safety of residents in a small town in Arkansas is in question after a man is murdered and when CJD seems to be passing through the residents of the town - something which is impossible unless the disease is consumed by mouth, or is there a strange case of cannibalism, similar to that of the ancient Anasazi tribe, circulating the town?

X Scully claims at one point to have a sample of Paula's brain cells. This is impossible, unless Scully had cut her skull open, which she evidently had not done.
Continuity

X Well, after the huge beef-scare here in the UK, it is now commonly known that it takes a few years for evidence of CJD to develop in body cells. In the episode, it occurs after a few weeks, which is highly inaccurate, though Mulder and Scully would be part of a very long investigation if the episode was accurate. (I'd give 'em the benefit of the doubt for that one.)
Plot Discrepancy

Recurring Actors: Hrothgar Matthews, Gabrielle Miller, Robin Mossley, Carrie Cain Sparks, Timothy Webber

Best Line: "She claims that she saw some kind of 'foxfire' spirit. I'm surprised she didn't call Oprah as soon as she got off the phone with the police" - Scully while explaining the case to Mulder.

Title Explanation: "This is our town." Is what Chaco said when he claimed that the town was to be defended from Mulder and Scully.

"Anasazi" (Part one of three)

Acomputer hacker makes away with some highly sensitive government files which detail knowledge of UFO's. They find their way to Mulder who ends up against government powers who want to stop him at all costs.

✗ In the first scene, with Mulder and The Lone Gunmen, a gunshot is heard from another apartment in Mulder's block and he rushes out to see what is going on, and finds that an elderly lady in a nearby apartment just shot her husband. The police arrive about ten seconds later. Now I know they're trying to reduce response time, but isn't that a little too fast a response? Even for a TV show?
Continuity

✗ Scully is called before the authorities of the FBI (note that the third man is show creator, Chris Carter) and she is questioned and tells the group that she has been working with Mulder for a year and a half. The first episode of The X-Files, which is Scully and Mulder's first case together, takes place on March 6th 1992, three years before April 1995 when this episode takes place. Of course, by the end of the second season, they had only spent two years working together, due to their separation and Scully's abduction, but this still suggests that Scully's claim of a year and a half is wrong. She must be really enjoying her work with Mulder to lose track of time...
Continuity

✗ When Mulder and Scully find that the government files are encrypted in Navajo, she says she'll try to find out what the files actually say. So, Scully visits a Navajo code talker. When Scully goes to

leave the office after speaking with the code-talker, the reflection of the boom-microphone can be seen in the glass frame of a picture on the wall opposite her.
Continuity

X Scully enters Mulder's apartment block basement to investigate after she witnesses deliveries of soft water. Here's the problem: many apartment blocks have soft water delivered, so why was she so suspicious?
Plot Discrepancy

X Scully later claims to have found dialysis canisters in the water tanks which probably had some kind of hallucinogenic inside, causing the strange behaviour in Mulder and the occupants of his apartment block. The new tank, which Scully took the canister out of, only had two small taps at the top: how did she get the large canister (which she showed to Mulder) out of such small holes? Cut the tank open with an FBI issued penknife?
Plot Discrepancy

X Towards the end of the episode, Scully shoots Mulder. (She later explains that she did this to stop him killing Krycek, with Krycek's gun, as it would frame Mulder for the death of his father.) After her point-blank shot we hear that someone is calling the police, so how did Scully make away with the body of an unconscious man who is almost a foot taller than her? And remember, the police in this episode had a very quick response time!
Plot Discrepancy

X In the final scenes, at the buried box-car, the area around the top hatch to the car is covered with a small amount of dirt, this can be seen when

Mulder and Eric open the hatch. However, when the troops arrive at the box-car, and Eric slams the hatch shut, the top has been cleaned off and a short length of the box-car's top side can be seen and looks as if it has been cleaned.

Continuity

Recurring Actors: Nicholas Lea, Paul McLean, Renea Morriseau

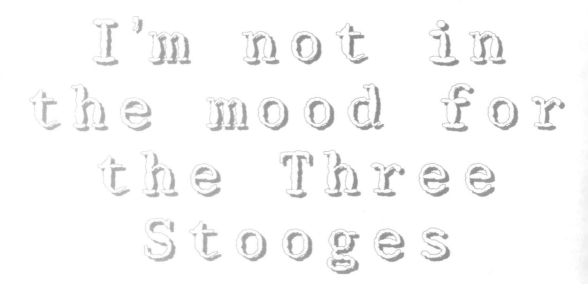

Best Line: "I'm not in the mood for the Three Stooges" - Mulder to the Lone Gunmen trio that turn up at his apartment unexpectedly.

Title Explanation: As Albert Hosteen explained, the Anasazi were a lost Indian tribe. "Anasazi" means "ancient aliens" and could also refer to the bodies found in the box-car as they were alien (in appearance, at least) and were almost ancient.

I'm not in
the mood for
the Three
Stooges

SEASON TWO "FAMILY SCORECARD"

DANA SCULLY: During and after her abduction, Dana's caring mother made a moving appearance - certain of her return. When she did come back Melissa Scully made an appearance, but Dana's brothers are presumed AWOL (they must really care about Dana).

FOX MULDER: The infinite strangeness of the Mulder family was seen again when Samantha Mulder turned up - but was unfortunately a clone, who Mulder lost with few clues. We finally got to meet his parents, who are now divorced. Mrs Mulder was unsure of the fake Sam's credibility, and William Mulder seemed cold and bitter. Unfortunately, Mulder sustained another loss - that of his father, murdered by Alex Krycek - at the end of the season.

"GET A LIFE!"

There has been a constant plea by fans of the show, on and off the Internet, that Scully and Mulder get given a personal life by the writers. While the writers are reluctant to get heavy on the details, the plea seems to have been granted in various tiny snippets throughout the series, but it still seems that Mulder and Scully really do spend most of their time just looking into X-files.

Outside work we have seen Dana Scully do various things. They are:

✗ Read a book, "Breakfast at Tiffany's", for example.
"War of the Coprophages"

✗ Clean her gun (okay this sort of comes under FBI work, but why not do it during her time off?)
"War of the Coprophages"

✗ Clean her dog.
"War of the Coprophages"

✗ Eat well, preferring a nice healthy salad.
"War of the Coprophages"

✗ Eat badly, preferring to eat ice cream straight from the tub. (A real woman said an on-line phile).
"War of the Coprophages"

✗ Sleep with her phone.
"War of the Coprophages"

✗ Surf the 'net.
"Die Hands Die Verletzt" and "War of the Coprophages"

X Walk to her mother's house shoeless and in despair, despite the fact she has a car (although you must remember she had lost Mulder at the time).
"The Blessing Way"

X Watch classic movies, those mentioned being "The Exorcist" and an unidentified Laurel and Hardy movie.
"Miracle Man", "Clyde Bruckman's Final Repose"

X And Scully has friends other than family members and Mulder, they are:
Cathy, who was going to the cello recital where Scully was shot **["Young at Heart"]**.
Jack Willis who was possessed by a bank robber **["Lazarus"]**.
Tom Coulton whose peers classed her as Mrs Spooky **["Squeeze"]**.

We have also seen Mulder do various things (but not as many as Scully, I might add).

X He watches old science-fiction movies.
Various episodes

X Keeps fit by running and swimming.
"Pilot", "Deep Throat", "Duane Barry", and "Humbug"

X Follow up UFO reports when he has nothing better to do (or better yet, when he can't go back to his apartment block because it is being fumigated). Were we to expect anything else?
"War of the Coprophages"

✗ "Hound" women, namely Dr. Bambi Barenbaum, and Detective White and has been known to ask someone to lunch and then not show up.
"War of the Coprophages", "Little Green Men"

✗ Write up case reports when at home (i.e. during his time off)
"War of the Coprophages"

✗ And porn is a regular habit of his.
You don't expect me to list all the occurrences do you? I do have a space limit y'know.

Season Three

"The Blessing Way" (Part two of three)

With Mulder's life in question, Scully returns to Washington D.C and is reprimanded for her previous actions. An encounter at Mulder's father's funeral and an incident involving the FBI entrance's metal detector reveals more about Scully's abduction and the government plans to silence her for good.

X When the box-car burns in the teaser, during Albert Hosteen's voice-over, we see that the set up for the box-car top, exposed from the dirt, was obviously not made of metal. It can be seen that it is made of plastic which is wrinkling from the heat of the fire, and at one point the plastic itself is catching fire!

Plot Discrepancy

X In the previous episode, **"Anasazi"**, Scully was shot at by persons unknown (we never found out who that was by the way), which caused her to be grazed across the head. However, the graze keeps disappearing and reappearing all through the early scenes of this episode, and is never seen again after she arrives back in Washington DC.

Recurring Actors: Forbes Angus, Alf Humphreys, Nicholas Lea

Best Line: As I said before, Mulder always seems to be able to crack a funny even in the most important of times:

Albert: "You must be careful now to end the ceremony properly. If you leave, you must not do any work, change clothes, or bathe for four days."

Mulder: "That's really gonna cut into my social life."

Also, a key passage taken from Albert's monologue during the episode - "While History serves only Those who seek to control it, those who would douse the Flame of Memory, in order to put out the danger Fire of Truth: beware these men, for they are dangerous themselves and unwise. Their false history is written in the blood of those who might remember - and of those who seek the Truth" - is all too true in the X-Files Universe.

Scenes: This episode also had a scene missing that was in the script, featuring Scully, her sister and her mother. The scene comes immediately after Scully walks to her mother's house and shows us that Scully blames herself for Mulder's death. Melissa then tells Dana that Mulder is still alive - she can sense it in Scully's feelings - but Scully says that Melissa doesn't know anything about her feelings.

Title Explanation: As mentioned by Albert Hosteen during his voice-overs, "The Blessing Way" was the chant and ceremony carried out by the Indians to heal Mulder and revive him.

History serves only Those who seek to control it

"Paper Clip" (Part three of three)

Mulder and Scully, now escaping powerful government forces, are led to a secret and abandoned government facility built into a mountain, which sheds more light on the abductions of Scully and Samantha Mulder. Meanwhile, Skinner tries to use the Digital Tape to strike a deal with the Cigarette-Smoking Man to reinstate Mulder and Scully.

✘ I couldn't help but find a nit-pick in the opening scenes (one of the best X-Files cliff hangers to date in my humble opinion). At the close of **"The Blessing Way"**, Scully and Skinner enter Mulder's apartment, and it is clear to the viewer that the blinds at the window are open - we can see the X that Mulder taped on in **"Anasazi"**. Yet, when the action begins again in **"Paper Clip"** the blinds are now drawn - no X is visible. I want to know who called time out during the showdown to make sure they had their privacy - Scully or Skinner?

Continuity

✘ I have no idea how Scully and Mulder got into the mine using the code "27828", as that isn't Napier's constant. The number she should have used is "27182" (Napier's constant = 2.71828).

Subject Matter

✘ In **"Conduit"** we are told that Samantha Mulder's middle name began with a T, in this episode, we are told her middle name is Ann.

Continuity

✘ **"Conduit"** also tells us that Samantha Mulder's birth date is 1/22/64 (January 22nd

1964), but we are told that her birth date is now 11/21/65 (November 21st 1965).
Continuity

✘ Also, Mulder's birthday changes from 10/11/60 (October 11th 1960) to 10/13/61 (October 13th 1961). (I am more willing to take this date, and the one above, as the actual dates for Fox and Samantha's birthdates as they are the "magical dates" that Chris Carter uses throughout the show.)
Continuity

✘ During The X-Files, we have seen that the government will stop at nothing to keep something secret, so why did such a highly protected government storage facility have a back door? Obviously it was just a plot device to make sure Mulder and Scully would safely escape, but why was it so easy to leave one way where you needed security codes (or, as Mulder suggested, "a small thermonuclear device") for huge electronic doors at the entrance?
Plot Discrepancy

✘ Also, when Mulder runs outside through this very back door to see the UFO, he leaves the door open. When he goes back inside, the door is closed, and he has to open it again.
Continuity

✘ Day-time goes on holiday again when the UFO appears (see **"Deep Throat"** and **"Ascension"** for similar incidents). We could see that it was a bright day when Mulder and Scully arrived at the mine, and they are only in there for a few moments when the UFO appears along with the "Black Ops". Suddenly it's night-time when Mulder witnesses the UFO and during their subsequent escape.
Continuity

✗ Mulder and Scully had to leave their car behind after escaping the mine, which probably meant that they left their map behind in the car (they weren't carrying it when they went in). They then run to a diner as we find later, but how did they know where they were? Even Skinner said the place wasn't on the map...
Continuity

✗ Later in the episode, Skinner tells Scully and Mulder that he was unable to make any kind of copy of the files on the tape. If this was the case where did Scully get the paper copies that she had in **"Anasazi"** and **"The Blessing Way"**?
Continuity

✗ At the end, Skinner tells the Cigarette-Smoking Man that Albert knows everything written on that tape. If this was the case, why didn't Albert tell Mulder and Scully what was on the tape? Maybe the fact Albert did not tell them was just to show that Skinner really was bluffing in his deal with the Cigarette-Smoking Man.
Plot Discrepancy

✗ And why does everyone keep referring to the tape as a DAT? It isn't a DAT. In fact it's a tape commonly used for backing up computer systems, and the only way to read the data from it is to use a backup program also never seen in this trilogy. (Then again, that could account for Skinner's previous claim - he wasn't using the correct program to read the tape, and had to take the information off it first.)
Subject Matter

Recurring Actors: Martin Evans, Nicholas Lea, Robert Lewis

Best Line: "Lots and lots of files" - Scully to Mulder after they find what is hidden in the secret mine.

Scenes: This is a great final part, well written, as with the rest of the trilogy, tense, and brilliantly acted. It is a shame that another family member was lost, but the final scene in the hospital is very touching, Scully's final lines seem to echo her quest in Season Three (as it seems she had more screen-time than ever - not that that's a bad thing): "I've seen the truth, now what I want are the answers."

Title Explanation: The title is taken from the Paper Clip Operation which occurred at the end of World War 2 and smuggled AXIS scientists into America. It is mentioned by Byers, one of the Lone Gunman, early in the episode.

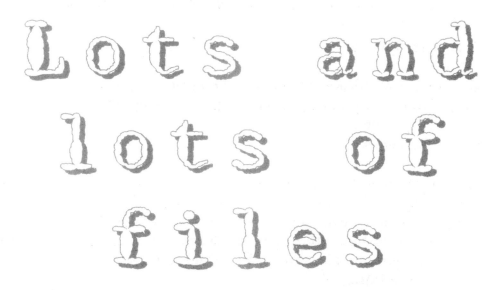

"D.P.O"

L ightening strikes are the subject of this episode, and they are all occurring in the same town, which is statistically improbable. Only one person in town has survived an attack, a boy named Darren Oswald, and he may be suffering from side-effects...

✗ "After everything we've been through..." - while trying to portray some sense of continuity between the previous saga, there is a slight problem. According to the date on the video game the episode was set in August, and **"Paper Clip"**, the previous episode, was set in April. Either the duo took a lot off time off to cope with their losses, and did not investigate any cases in the three months between the cases, or lost their memories.

Continuity

✗ And staying with the date on the video game, do they really store the time and date? The date maybe, but definitely not the time.

Subject Matter

✗ Some music heard throughout the episode is by the British group James, and another song was "Hey Man, Nice Shot" by Filter.

Music Moments

✗ If Darren had really survived three lightning strikes, wouldn't there be at least some sign of it? His hair may have been affected for example (however, if the effects/make-up people had Darren's hair affected then it would have looked plain silly).

Continuity

X We find later in the story that Darren has an obsession with a teacher from his school and Mulder and Scully find a picture of the teacher in Darren's bedroom. The picture is torn from a yearbook, but the information about the pictured teacher is printed on the back of the photo. As the picture was from a yearbook, shouldn't the name and other information about the pictured person be printed underneath, not on the next page?
Plot Discrepancy

Recurring Actors: Mar Andersons, Bonnie Hay, Steve Makaj

Best Line: "The tread looks like a standard military boot... men's... size eight and a half." Is Scully psychic? Unfortunately, no.

Title Explanation: "DPO" are the initials of the main focus of the episode, Darren Peter Oswald. They were seen by Mulder on a video game machine scoreboard.

"Clyde Bruckman's Final Repose"

Scully and Mulder become involved in an investigation regarding the deaths of several psychics. They encounter Clyde Bruckman, who finds another victim and knows more about the murders than was released to the press. Mulder thinks Bruckman is psychic, and can help them solve the case, but the power Bruckman has is a bit more specific...

X The on-screen legends tell us that the events in this episode involving Scully and Mulder begin on the date of September 19th and finish on September 22nd. Unfortunately, Bruckman's lotto ticket says otherwise - placing the date of the draw on October 9th. It's impossible really... as he would be dead! (I place a bit more confidence in the on-screen legends, despite the fact the lotto ticket is part of the events. But although I say that, the **"Clyde Bruckman's Final Repose"** script does say the postmark of the letter sent by The Puppet is dated October 9th, which is the day of the draw.)
Continuity

X Unfortunately, despite the fact I don't think anyone would like to see it, Bruckman isn't naked in the vision of his own death, as he describes. And later, when he does die, with Scully holding his hand compassionately and the tear falling down his face (though I think Scully would have Rationally Explained it as a random drop of condensation), he isn't naked. (This is one nit-pick that isn't worth fretting over, just an observation.)
Continuity

Recurring Actors: Alex Diakun, Dwight McFee, David McKay, Ken Roberts

Best Line: As I said with **"Humbug"**, Darin Morgan episodes are the funniest of the bunch, you cannot expect me to pinpoint one.

Title Explanation: The title refers to Clyde Bruckman's final prediction of someone's death. Namely that of his own. Clyde Bruckman's name is taken from that of a silent movie director of the 1930's - Darin Morgan is a huge fan of silent movies.

3X05

"The List"

Adeath row prisoner, Leech Manley is executed, and claims he will return and kill five people who had made him suffer. A while after the electrocution a murder occurs at the prison, and Mulder investigates, thinking there may be some truth in Manley's claim.

X During Mulder and Scully's first visit to a high security prison full of dangerous convicts Scully is left alone in an empty cell, and even manages to wander off on her own for a while (and encounters the hiding guard who tells her that Roach has the list). Would the guard really leave her alone? Even if this is Scully - an armed FBI agent - there was a killer on the loose.
Plot Discrepancy

X Why would Scully be so sceptical about reincarnation, seeing as she's encountered the phenomenon twice already? (In **"Lazarus"** and **"Born Again"**.)
Continuity

Recurring Actors: Craig Brunanski, Mitchell Kosterman

"Best Line: Scully questions the reincarnation theory, but not in her usual sceptical way:

> Mulder: "Imagine if it were true, Scully. Imagine if you could come back and take out five people who had caused you to suffer. Who would they be?"
> Scully: "I only get five?"
> Mulder: "I remembered your birthday this year didn't I, Scully?" "

Title Explanation: Leech Manley was said to have a list of five people he would return to after death and kill, the title refers to this list.

3X06

"2shy"

A serial killer who has a strange bodily deficiency uses on-line computer networks to lure in his victims. Mulder and Scully are called in when one of these victims is found, covered with a strange substance that seems to be capable of dissolving the body's fatty tissue.

✗ Again, Scully's sense of time is off. She dates the autopsy as August 29th, but the episodes **"Clyde Bruckman's Final Repose"** and **"The List"** both took place before this episode and were set in September. Also, during the autopsy she says that it is 4:15 p.m., the clock on the wall reads differently. And finally, the August date is contradicted when the DNA test is dated October 27.
Continuity

✗ When Mulder talks to the first victim's room mate she tells him that the victim was a user of on-line services, which is how she met 2shy. Mulder then asks to use the phone to call Scully, and when talking to Scully he says that he has already spoken to the on-line service. (This would be explained if a scene involving Mulder speaking with the management of the on-line service had been cut from the episode.)

Plot Discrepancy

✗ The computer technician claims that he was able to find the possible list of targets by looking at Encanto's computer hard drive. We are told that the hard drive itself had been reformatted, meaning that it had been wiped clean, but the technician says he is able to restore the lost files. The only problem is, how could he retrieve something that wasn't there?

Plot Discrepancy

✗ Why did Ellen lock Encanto in her apartment after being so worried about being near him?

Plot Discrepancy

✗ After the strange occurrences at the lab, with the corpse that has almost melted, Scully tells Mulder that the substance used to cause decay in the fatty tissue was stomach acid, but twice as strong. If it was strong enough to cause almost-instant breakdown of flesh, how was Scully able to pull the substance out of Ellen's mouth and off her face without it eating away at her own flesh?

Plot Discrepancy

Recurring Actors: Glynis Davies, William MacDonald, Kerry Sandomirsky

Best Line: "OK, it's not yet the finely detailed insanity that you've come to expect from me, but..." - Mulder.

Title Explanation: "2shy" was the handle, or nickname, used by Encanto on the Internet. (He also used "Timid".)

3X07

"The Walk"

A soldier trying to commit suicide claims that a strange phantom is stopping him from committing the act and is trying to destroy his life by keeping him alive, and killing all those close to him. Scully and Mulder listen to his case, with Scully finding it to be typical shell-shock trauma, while Mulder believes the story. As they investigate, they find that the military has not disclosed certain facts on the case, and meet opposition from the same powers.

X When the case is being attacked by Callahan, he says it is a criminal investigation, despite the fact there is no criminal element to the case. (Which even begs the question: why the FBI involvement?)
Continuity

X Callahan hears the strange voice on his answer machine in his office, muttering the words "killer", and later tells Mulder and Scully. He tells the agents that the phantom knows his name, yet the phantom never said his name.
Continuity

✗ If the military is so keen to keep the suicide attempt and the previous deaths quiet, and have accomplished this to some extent, how did Mulder and Scully find out about the case?
Continuity

✗ And would Scully really act that way towards a General? May be she only respects those of a Navy background. Or she's been hanging around with Mulder for too long and has developed a heavy disrespect for the military.
Plot Discrepancy

Recurring Actors: Deryl Hayes, Don Thompson, Beatrice Zeilinger

Best Line: "I guess this isn't a good time to thank you for seeing us" - Mulder after being warned against FBI involvement.

Title Explanation: The walk was the journey the projected form - or phantom soldier - of Trimble went on to claim its victims.

"Oubliette"

Ayoung girl, Amy Jacobs, is kidnapped from her home in the middle of the night - Mulder takes interest as, although he doesn't mention it, he parallels the case with that of his sister's disappearance. As he and Scully investigate, they are led to Lucy Householder, a lady kidnapped in the same way over two decades ago, but who may have some connection with the latest abduction, though not as an accomplice.

X Mulder tells Scully that Lucy was kidnapped at the age of eight. With Lucy being thirty years old now, that would make it twenty-two years ago, yet later on, he says it was fifteen years ago.
Continuity

X Was it wise of Mulder to tell Wade to "Hold it right there!" when he has Amy's head underwater?
Continuity

X What was the deal with abandoning Amy like that when she was pulled from the water? Scully says that they should abandon her, when it is quite commonly known that victims of drowning can be resuscitated up to forty-five minutes later. And both Mulder and Scully, wearing nice warm, heavy trench-coats, forget to wrap the girl up in one of them and keep her warm. (And Scully calls herself a doctor...)
Plot Discrepancy

Recurring Actors: David Fredericks, Bonnie Hay, David Lewis

Best Line: Another Mulder and Scully exchange:
Scully: "That's spooky…"
Mulder: "That's my name, isn't it?"

Title Explanation: An oubliette is an underground prison where the only entrance is a small opening at the top. An oubliette was what both girls were held in during their kidnappings. The name is from the French word "oublier", meaning "to forget"; a prisoner would be thrown in this underground cage and forgotten about.

3X09

"Nisei" (Part one of two)

Mulder and Scully find themselves investigating another conspiracy when Mulder buys a tape of an alien autopsy. Scully believes the tape is almost as fake as the one showed on television but Mulder believes it is authentic because it doesn't reveal too much. As they track down the tape's distributor, a plot involving Japanese scientists is begun along with the revealing of some information regarding Scully's abduction.

X Mulder doesn't appear to be paying attention to what the Senator tells him about the deaths of the Japanese scientists. Matheson tells Mulder that they were killed two weeks ago in Knoxville, Tennessee, but Mulder later tells Scully they died yesterday.
Continuity

X While the pictures of the Talapus were very convincing and realistic looking, they were

actually fake; having been taken from famous pictures
of a real-life boat, the Bismark.

Subject Matter

Recurring Actors: Roger Allford, Gillian
Barber, Paul McLean, Carrie Cain Sparks, Bob
Wilde

Best Line: "I get tired of losing my gun" -
Mulder to the Japanese Senate member after his gun
has been knocked out of his hands; the line was put
in as Mulder's constant dropping of his gun was con-
tinually joked about by fans on the Internet. (His running gun-drop total so far: fourteen up until the end of
Season Three.)

Scenes: The scene with Scully and the other abductees
sticks in my mind, or the "tupperware party from hell", as
it has been classed.

Title Explanation: The scientists in the episode
were Nisei, which was to be an American or Canadian
born of Japanese immigrant parents.

"731" (Part two of two)

The story from "Nisei" continues as Mulder becomes trapped on train 82517 carrying some very live cargo. Scully must race to save him as she meets a dubious government official and more hidden government experiments.

X The opening scene - all those hybrids/lepers being shot - was chilling, but had a strange legacy which didn't appear when Scully was shown the graves. All the beings were shot, which means that there must have been bullet wounds, yes? If that's the case, where did the bullet wounds go? I didn't see any...
Continuity

X Scully speeds to Mulder's apartment (driving very erratically, by the way), and places a masking-taped X on his window for assistance from X. As she does this (carelessly pushing those books to the floor - messy Dana) we get a good look at Mulder's desk. Does anyone else find it weird that Mulder has a computer keyboard, but no CPU or monitor? No wonder they call him Spooky.
Continuity

X Those pages of writing in the notebooks seen throughout were very authentic looking, and were written in real Japanese. It's just a shame that Mulder or the translator didn't notice that all the pages of the books were identical. (Obviously just the prop department's way of saving money, and very undetectable - I noticed it by accident.)
Continuity

X I personally loved the closing scene - I want to know what the Cigarette-Smoking Man isn't involved in - but I couldn't help but find a nit-pick. We open with the translator, who is reading the Japanese notes and copying them out in English, he wears glasses and in a reflection in the eye-wear we see a match lit up. The camera angle changes, and we see that the match lighter, the Cigarette-Smoking Man, is standing quite a space away from the translator. So, how was there a perfectly clear and large reflection in the glass, when the match was over two metres away, and when the glasses were tilted down and not up towards the match?

Recurring Actors: Colin Cunningham, Michael Puttonen

Best Line: "Why did I study French in high school?" - Mulder, after finding that the doctor's notes on alien/human hybrids are written in Japanese.

Title Explanation: The 731 was a military unit mentioned by Mulder in **"Nisei"** which the scientists operated in. They performed experiments on civilians.

"Revelations"

The death of several fake stigmatics, those suffering from wounds identical to those inflicted on Jesus Christ at the crucifixion, leads Scully to believe that Mulder's investigation into these false prophets has turned up a real one - an eleven year old boy. While Scully's Catholic background causes her to believe in this miracle, Mulder is more sceptical, finding no truth in the claim.

X Would social services really remove Kevin from his mother's care when it was obvious she had not caused the wounds he displayed at school? The whole class and the teacher could see that he didn't come in bleeding, and the sudden wounds shocked them all, so why make the sudden jump in logic to the accusation that his mother was to blame?

Plot Discrepancy

Recurring Actors: Cecere Fulvio, Lesley Exen

Best Line: "Would you smell Mr Jarvis?"- Scully to Mulder during Owen Jarvis' autopsy when she thinks the body smells of flowers.

Scenes: Did you think that Mulder was being slightly insensitive during this episode? Well, a line during his and Scully's final scene together could have outweighed all this. In an earlier copy of the script he tells Scully that they have a few hours before their plane leaves, and says something to the effect of: "It's been a long time since we've done something together, why don't we go to a movie or something?" Scully tells him she has an errand to run and we have the brilliant scene at the end. It's a shame that that one hit the cutting room floor.

Title Explanation: A revelation is divine communication of some kind, in this instance in the form of Kevin the stigmatic, and, as Scully says, God may be speaking, but no one is listening.

3X12

"War of the Coprophages"

Mulder takes time off while his apartment block is being fumigated to investigate some UFO sightings in Grover's Mill, New Jersey. While there he becomes involved in a case of cockroach-related deaths, drawing Scully in through a regular bout of phone calls, who eventually comes down to join the investigation.

X So Doctor Eckerle is "Chief Science Officer"? Isn't that a designation used in "Star Trek"?
Subject Matter

X At the end of the episode, when Mulder and Scully "look pooped", there is a spate of troubles with Miss Scully's hair. At one point, as Eckerle talks with the duo and Bambi, Scully's hair (all loose and flustered because of the wind and her previous escape from the waste dump) irritates her to such an extent that she reaches up to brush it away. As she does, the scenes changes to a shot behind her, and her arm is still down. When the shot shows her face again, her hair is still covering her forehead - either a mixing of takes, or she had no luck pushing it away. When Eckerle and Bambi walk away together, Scully's hair changes and is now all nice and neat. (Smart, sexy and perfect hair…)
Continuity

Recurring Actors: Bill Dow, Tom Heaton, Maria Herrera, Ken Kramer, Bobby L. Stewart

" Best Line: "Are you sure it wasn't a girlie scream?"- Scully to Mulder after he tells her of his insect fear and how he freaked out when he saw a praying mantis. **"**

Title Explanation: The title gives a nod to two things; along with the town where the episode took place (Grover's Mill being a mix-up of "War of the World's" Miller's Grove), it is the H.G. Wells' book "War of the Worlds". Coprophages are dung-eating beetles, but in this case they are dung-eating cockroaches.

Are you sure it wasn't a girlie scream?

"Syzygy"

A death allegedly committed by Satanists takes Mulder and Scully to the town of Comity, the town of harmony. As more murders occur, Mulder finds that there may be another cause which is having strange effects on everyone in the town - changing their moods and personality. Even Scully and Mulder cannot escape the event, which has also had its effect on two girls...

X The time on the legend when Scully arrives at the scene of the second murder - the boy being crushed by the bleachers - says 5:10 a.m. A.M? If the murder was a few hours ago, when was the practice session? Three in the morning?
Continuity

X And while at the second murder scene, Scully's sense of timing seems off again, this time saying that Mulder and her have been working together for two years, when it's now four.
Continuity

X Recognise the song playing when the two girls are in the burger bar with the boy who eventually is killed by a flying spring? It's "Deep" by Danzig, a song featured on The X-Files' inspired music album, "Songs in the Key of X".
Music Moment

X Astronomical objects do not move according to earthbound time schedules, so it is highly unlikely that the alignment would have reached its peak at 12 midnight. (However, it could have happened, just being coincidence.)
Subject Matter

X Also, the powers and attitudes forced upon the people in Comity would have grown gradually, as the alignment neared perfection, reached their peak, and then died down gradually as the alignment broke apart. As soon as the alignment was completed, and became fractionally out of line, the cosmic forces it created would not stop, as it would contradict the way the forces came into being.

Continuity

Recurring Actors: Garry Davey, Tim Dixon, Gabrielle Miller, Denalda Williams

Best Lines: "Sure, fine, whatever." Spoken by both Mulder and Scully throughout the episode.

Also:

Scully: "Why do you always have to drive? Because you're the guy? Because you're the big, macho man?"
Mulder: "No. I was just never sure your little feet could reach the pedals."

(Strangely enough, Scully has driven the car in the show when with Mulder, namely in **"Fresh Bones"** and **"Clyde Bruckman's Final Repose"**. She should be suspicious though, as both times this was used simply as a plot device.)

Title Explanation: The Syzygy is the planetary alignment in this episode.

"Grotesque"

John Mostov, who has committed a string of murders where the body is heavily mutilated, is finally caught and apprehended by Agent Bill Patterson, an old teacher of Mulder's. When Mostov claims to have been possessed by a gargoyle that caused him to murder, Mulder is called in to help the investigations under Skinner's order. As Mulder and Scully investigate, with Patterson and Mulder disagreeing on Mostov's claims, the murders continue, even with Mostov in prison.

✗ In John Mostov's cell, Scully asks why he is on the floor, to which Mulder replies "He's been working", and points at a sketch of a gargoyle on the floor. Mostov was wearing a straight-jacket, how did he draw with his hands held down?
Continuity

✗ And what did Mostov draw on the floor with? I doubt he'd be allowed a pencil or even chalk in his cell.
Plot Discrepancy

✗ Scully has been hanging around with Mulder too long; when the cat jumps out at her in Mostov's "studio" she says "I thought it was one of those pictures coming to life." Very un-Scully-like; unless we just saw through a crack in her scientific armour? (Or she's been working with Mulder for way too long.)
Continuity

✗ Scully can drive fast! She manages to make it to the studio after talking on the phone with Mulder in two minutes flat. Speedy.
Continuity

Recurring Actors: None

Best Line: "I saw your new wallpaper" - Scully to Mulder after taking a peek inside his apartment to find it littered with Mostov's gargoyle drawings. (Makes you wonder if she is just freely allowed to walk into his apartment all the time.)

Title Explanation: Grotesque is an older label for gargoyles, the subject of this episode, due to their strange, horrific shaping.

how did he draw with his hands held down?

"Piper Maru" (Part one of two)

Skinner informs Scully that the investigation into her sister's murder is to be shut down due to lack of evidence and being a waste of time, Scully says it is because the government is not interested and storms away. Scully finds Mulder in the basement office looking into the case of the boat "Piper Maru" which seems to have encountered what could be a UFO. Mulder and Scully investigate, and spark off a strange sequence of events.

✗ We see that Mulder has no gun, as this is Hong Kong, and they're banned. So why did everyone else have theirs?
Continuity

✗ Krycek has apparently been selling secrets from the digital tape of the previous episodes of **"Anasazi"**, **"The Blessing Way"**, and **"Paper Clip"**. There are two problems; we learn in the next episode, **"Apocrypha"**, that the tape had been in a locker in the US all along. So how did Krycek sell the information if he didn't have the tape? And he cannot have had a hard copy on paper or another tape because Skinner told us in **"Paper Clip"** that it was uncopyable. Secondly, the tape was written in Navajo, and Scully claimed in **"Anasazi"** that there was only a handful of people left who could read it, so how did Krycek read it? Does he have an English-Navajo dictionary? Or was he taking night classes when on the run?
Continuity & Plot Discrepancy

✗ In the next episode, the ever-smokey Cigarette-Smoking Man tells the Well-Manicured Man that whoever shot Skinner was "working on his own", which was most probably untrue - the Cigarette-Smoking Man is desperate to get rid of Skinner -

but would Cardinal's orders have been to leave any evidence? (Let alone witnesses, as he does with the waitress.) I don't think so, but that's exactly what he does when he spits on Skinner. However, if Cardinal was acting on his own, and it is a possibility, why would he just shoot Skinner anyway? He can't have been that angry over a few coins. (And Walter takes a lot of wounds this season... don't you think?)
Plot Discrepancy

X Any reason why Scully was the contact address if Skinner was in a medical emergency? Wouldn't it have been more appropriate if Sharon Skinner, the wife we learn he has in **"Avatar"**, was alerted? Okay, so they has been separated some time, but she was still his next of kin, which Scully definitely isn't (unless there's something going on between the two off-camera that we haven't been told about). My SRE (Scully Rational Explanation) is that it was the FBI-gossip ringing Scully, and we just never saw Sharon.
Continuity and Plot Discrepancy

Recurring Actors: Paul Batten, Robert Clothier, Nicholas Lea, Morris Paynch

Best Line: Scully manages to class Mulder's position in the basement while cracking a joke:

Scully: "I'm just constantly amazed by you. You're working down here in the basement sifting through files and transmissions that any other agent would just throw away in the garbage."
Mulder: "Well that's why I'm in the basement, Scully."
Scully: "You're in the basement because they're afraid of you, of your relentlessness, and because

they know that they could drop you in the middle of the desert, and tell you the truth is out there, and you would ask them for a shovel."

Mulder: "Is that what you think of me?"

Scully: "Well, maybe not a shovel. Maybe a back-hoe."

Title Explanation: The boat featured in this episode is named the Piper Maru, but where does that name come from? Piper and Maru are Gillian Anderson's daughter's first and second names. The name is obviously an inside joke, maybe because Chris Carter is Piper's godfather, and Carter is always using his and his wife's birth date in numbers throughout the show.

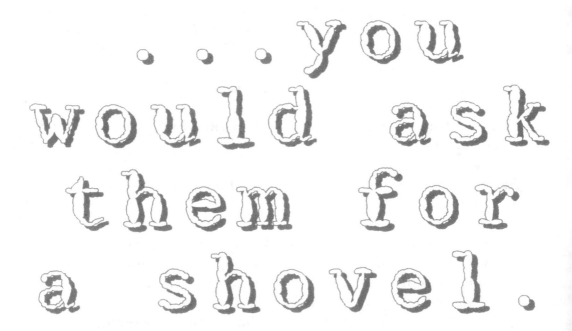

. . . you would ask them for a shovel.

"Apocrypha" (Part two of two)

The story continues from "Piper Maru" as Scully searches for clues to Skinner's shooting, and eventually finds a link she didn't expect. Meanwhile, Mulder returns to the US with Krycek in tow, who really does seem like a new man...

X When the mysterious Men In Black pull Krycek from the car, after it has been rammed off of the road, it can be clearly seen that Mulder is unconscious. He then comes to and witnesses the bright flash, but sees nothing more. But later on he tells Scully that he saw Krycek taken away. Mulder is very good at playing unconscious, but watching what is going on around him at the same time - with his eyes closed? I don't think so.
Continuity

X Scully makes a slight slip-up with what she says to Agent Pendrell as they discuss the sample retrieved from the scene of Skinner's shooting: "...we're looking for a male, probably in his 40's with blood type B positive, but we already know all that from the waitress' description." So the waitress can just look at a man and tell his blood type? That's not right...either that or she's in the wrong profession.
Continuity

X Psychic-Scully was very intuitive to take the PCR (DNA test) results from Pendrell, as it later helps her find that Skinner's shooter is also that of her sister Melissa's. I want to know where the PCRs from Melissa's shooter came from. Both Krycek and Luis Cardinal (or the "Hispanic Man" as he was known back then) were wearing gloves when

Melissa was shot (as you can see when the murder takes place in **"The Blessing Way"**), and Cardinal didn't make the stupid mistake of spitting on her; so where did the DNA sample come from which is needed to make a PCR?

`Continuity`

X The whole situation with the alien getting to Krycek is confusing to say the least. How did the alien know that it could get to its UFO through Krycek? It was trapped for so long under the sea that it wouldn't have known who Krycek was or his connection with the Consortium. This is a plot-hole where you just have to grit your teeth and give Chris Carter the benefit of the doubt.

`Plot Discrepancy`

X What's an "Advanced Life Support Unit"? Isn't it actually called an ambulance? (Watch when Scully runs to the ambulance Skinner is being carried away in.)

`Subject Matter`

X And why was Skinner alone in the ambulance?

`Plot Discrepancy`

Recurring Actors: Martin Evans, David Kaye, Nicholas Lea, Sue Mathew, Kevin McNulty

Best Line: "I'll be damned!" - Frohike, a member of the Lone Gunmen trio, after Mulder reveals that the high-tech instrument used to determine the writing on the envelope was a pencil. And of course, Gillian Anderson should be acknowledged/praised/awarded/(fill as applicable) for the scene where she finally stops Cardinal and almost kills him herself.

Scenes: One of the best scenes has to be with the Lone Gunmen at the ice-skating ring. I guess that they forgot what inconspicuous meant.

Title Explanation: The Apocrypha are books in some versions of the Bible, but "apocryphal" also means secret or hidden things, which is probably more applicable to this episode after what happens at the end when the business with the UFO is sorted out.

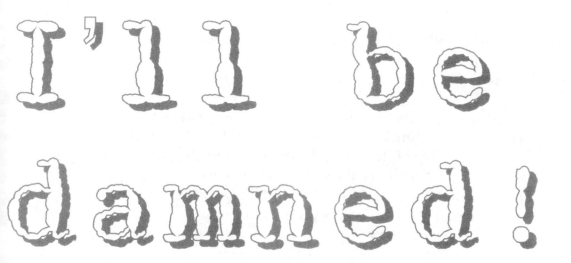

I'll be damned!

"Pusher"

After a killing spree lasting one year, FBI Frank Agent Burst finally thinks he has caught the man called "Pusher" who seems capable of forcing his will on others. Unfortunately, the Pusher uses his powers to escape, and Burst enlists the help of Scully and Mulder. As the agents track Pusher, he uses his powers to lead Mulder and Scully into a game of cat-and-mouse.

X The phone call with Burst and Pusher has few errors, as there is no need to trace the call. Already, telephone networks offer customers a service to tell them who called the phone last (or who the current caller is) and phone signals now carry the caller's number, so the method the SWAT team uses is quite old. Also, this is TV land, everyone in the team, along with Burst, Mulder and Scully, should have known that the number prefix would be 555!
Plot Discrepancy and Subject Matter

X Sticking with the phone-call scene: are Mulder and Scully - FBI Agents - really outranked by the SWAT officers? In essence, Mulder and Scully had as much power over the SWAT team as Burst had, so they would have been able to warn them of Pusher killing Burst, and order them to disconnect the phone line.
Plot Discrepancy

X For some strange reason, the entrance to the FBI building has changed since **"The Blessing Way"**. They've done away with that big plaque of the FBI logo on the floor and the ceiling has been dropped at the edges and raised at the centre.
Continuity

X There is a blatant set re-dressing when Model manages to bluff his way into the FBI building. The fourth floor corridor is exactly the same as the corridor that Skinner's office is located in. In fact, the computer records office is the mini-foyer for his office! No wonder Skinner was surprised to see the blinds drawn - his secretary had gone and a computer system was in her place!

`Continuity`

X Mulder enters the hospital, decked out in SWAT gear, and hears two shots fired in the background, he investigates, and finds five bullets in the floor. In fact, only two of those are empty, and the other three were taken out of the gun by Model, giving the brilliant tense Russian Roulette game at the end. But this isn't even mentioned by Mulder; I would have thought he might just acknowledge the bullets' existence as he is wearing the headset and reporting back what he finds.

`Continuity`

X After the first shooting, Scully points out (through the image gained from the camera) that Model has a mass in his right temple lobe as it is shown on a computer screen near Mulder. It was quite a leap to think this was Model's MIT scan, was it not? Even if it did turn out to be correct.

`Plot Discrepancy`

X There is some take-splicing here, when Scully goes to enter the hospital after Mulder encounters Pusher. She stops to talk to a SWAT officer first of all and from an angle at her right side, she is wearing her bullet-proof vest slightly crooked. When the camera changes angles, to her left side, she has it on straight.

`Continuity`

X Model says that he read in "her" files that Scully shot Mulder. Unfortunately, his story doesn't match with Skinner's. He never read "her" files, according to Skinner, having only accessed Mulder's, which is probably where the information came from. (Scully-esque Rational Explanation: the tumour must be playing havoc with his memory.)

Continuity

Recurring Actors: Steve Basic, Meredith Bain-Woodward, Roger Cross, Don MacKay

Best Line: "Please explain to me the scientific nature of the 'whammy'." - Scully to Mulder.

Title Explanation: As Frank Burst told Mulder and Scully, the Pusher could push his will on to others.

"Teso dos Bichos"

When artefacts are unearthed from the Ecuadorian highlands and sent to the US despite warnings against the act from the locals, deaths occur, leading Scully and Mulder to the case. While it appears that this could be political terrorism against the museum holding the relics, Mulder feels that the cause could be an unleashed jaguar spirit.

X Some of the police officers should really pay attention in this show (as should some of the supporting cast - never enter a toilet in The X-Files on your own!). The scene following the opening credits shows the professor finding the bloody scene and as he rushes off (presumably to call the police), the camera pans along, in a mysterious style, to reveal the urn sitting in the corner. Later, when Mulder and Scully arrive at the crime scene, someone has moved the urn, as Mona takes them to a different area of the museum to see it. Now surely, given that this is the scene of a crime, shouldn't it have not been disturbed? And anyhow, I doubt the police would let someone into the scene while they were still examining it.
Continuity

Recurring Actors: Tom McBeath, Alan Robertson, Ron Sauve

Best Line: "Go with it, Scully" - Mulder after being asked if *he* has been drinking the hallucinogen.

Scenes: It's interesting to note that there was a competition between the show's writers to see who would be the first to kill off QueegQueeg, Scully's dog, who we are to see next in

"Quagmire".   Even more interesting is that this episode originally had included the involvement of QueegQueeg, and the mutt's tragic death at the hands of the killer cats. Luckily, it was dropped from the final script and the demise of the dog was left for **"Quagmire"**.

Title Explanation: The title itself is Spanish for "hill of animals" or "mound of animals" which refers to the area disturbed in the episode.

"Hell Money"

The death of a Chinese immigrant during the festival of the Hungry Ghosts teams Mulder and Scully up with Detective Chao, a Chinese police officer who is battling between ancient tradition and the law to bring justice after the murders.

X Why were the creators selective in which segments of Chinese dialogue to subtitle? I would have liked to know what was said between Detective Chao and Mr Hsin for example. I know they like to keep us in the dark, but I thought that was just for the conspiracy...
Continuity

X Are Mulder and Scully deliberately showing off their new compact flashlights in this episode? Unfortunately, they aren't as powerful as the "good flashlights" Mulder spoke of in **"Apocrypha"**.

Recurring Actors: Doug Abrahams

Best Line: "No, but if I'm right, this is one man who left his heart in San Francisco" - Scully's quip over the latest victim.

Title Explanation: The "hell money" was the fake money used by the Chinese to ward off ghosts that were haunting the family.

"Jose Chung's 'From Outer Space'"

Scully is interviewed by Jose Chung, a writer who has decided to create a new writing genre - non-fiction science fiction - and she is to discuss a previous case involving alien abduction with him. As the interview progresses, with flashbacks to the case in question, it appears that facts have become severely distorted by everyone involved, leaving Chung with very different reports of events.

X Well, the chain of events have been skewed so badly that even Scully doesn't have the details correct! As she tells Chung, Chrissy awoke in the car to find her clothes on "inside-out and back-to-front". Unfortunately, as the following shots show us, Chrissy's clothes are not on back-to-front, as she fiddles with some buttons. (Unless of course, she has clothes which button up at the back, which I find unlikely.)
Continuity

X When Chrissy awakes in her bed to see the alien, which was a cat (if you follow my meaning), there are various close-up shots of her as she looks about her room, and eventually gets out of bed. During these shots, the bloodstain underneath her nose begins to fade in some shots, and even gets darker in others.
Continuity

140

Recurring Actors: Alex Diakun, Michael Dobson, Larry Musser

" Best Line: "Mulder, you're nuts!" - Scully finally tells Mulder "the truth", and "How the hell should I know?" - spoken by numerous people throughout. **"**

Scenes: The best has to be the alien autopsy video, hosted by the Stupendous Yappi himself - obviously Scully's worst nightmare to be associated with the thing. Also, Detective Manners' "colourful phraseology" was initially written without the bleeps, and with X-Files director Kim Manners playing the part due to his alleged lack of manners (hence the name). Unfortunately, the censors didn't like the language, so another actor, and overuse of the word "bleep", was drafted in.

Title Explanation: Fairly simple, no translations or hidden definitions, the episode is about Jose Chung who is interviewing Scully for research while writing his non-fiction-science-fiction book, eventually called "From Outer Space".

[**Note:** The original title for this episode was **"Eth Snafu"**, "Eth" being a mix up of the word "The", "Snafu" an originally military acronym meaning "Situation Normal, All Fouled (or F*cked) Up. This would have referred to the mix up of events in the episode.]

Darin Morgan broke a record with this episode, with the most in-jokes ever in an episode of The X-Files. Which is why I set aside this moment for a complete listing:

Jose Chung's "In-jokes"

1. How many other science-fiction films and TV shows did Darin hint at?

I. Film wise; there were hints at "Aliens" with the alien repeating "this is not happening".

II. The potato mashing of Lt. Shaffer, just like Richard Dreyfuss in "Close Encounters of the Third Kind'.

III. And then there is the big "Star Wars" reference at the beginning with the truck flying over the camera, much in the same way as a Star Destroyer did in the movie.

IV. For television there are numerous hints; "Space: Above and Beyond" being a TV series which episode writer Darin Morgan's brother, Glen, co-created (this hint was seen on Bliane's t-shirt).

V. There is also Mulder eating the pieces of pie in a very reminiscent way to "Twin Peaks" a show which has been addressed as one of the unintentional predecessors of The X-Files.

VI. There is a slight would-be reference to The X-Files when Chung says he wants to create his new genre - non-fiction, science-fiction.

VII. The appearance of Alex Trebeck, "Jeopardy" host, a show David Duchovny has appeared on (see the Jeopardy! page for more details).

VIII. And finally the alien autopsy, "Truth or Humbug?" which refers to both the past episodes of The X-Files (**"Humbug"**, for the title, **"Nisei"** and **"731"**, for their own alien autopsies) and the documentary of the very same nature on Fox Television.

2. How many references to The X-Files can Darin fit in?

I. The Stupendous Yappi, encountered by Mulder and Scully in **"Clyde Bruckman's Final Repose"**, turns up as the host of the alien autopsy video.

II. During the alien autopsy video and in some parts of the episode there was a tune very similar to the main theme for the show.

III. Mulder does have a girlie scream, as Scully said in **"War of the Coprophages"**, we learn this when he sees the dead "alien" body.

IV. Darin Morgan seems to prey on the "emotionless" portrayal of Mulder by Duchovny as he did in **"Humbug"**, with Blaine saying Mulder was a "mandroid" (this would also be a hint at Mulder's cameo in "Space: Above and Beyond" as an android).

V. Blaine has an "I WANT TO BELIEVE" poster on his wall, like Mulder's, but we can barely see the "WANT TO" on this version.

VI. The smoking alien? A bit reminiscent of the Cigarette-Smoking Man, perhaps?

VII. When she awakes suddenly, Chrissy mistakes her toy cat for an alien, a reference to **"Teso dos Bichos"**.

VIII. Also, changed names of Scully and Mulder in the final copy of Chung's book; Diana Lusky (an almost-anagram) and Reynard Muldrake ("reynard" being French for "fox").

3. How many references to X-Philes, and their X-Files questions, does Darin answer or hint at?

I. Some fans want to know if Mulder's apartment actually has a bedroom, and it would seem he does, as we see at the episode's end.

II. Some fans, usually Internet-based, want Mulder and Scully to become romantically involved, so in this episode, Mulder awakes in Scully's hotel room. (But not in the context the "relationshippers" would have liked.)

III. Many fans criticise the fact that Mulder and Scully rarely get any evidence, and luckily, Mulder has a man with a video camera at hand to film the alien autopsy. Unfortunately, the alien turns out not to be real and the video footage gets twisted and edited into something it isn't.

IV. Blaine himself said that Scully's hair was red, but a little too red, as many fans have also complained (obviously a dig at Gillian Anderson having to have her ash-blonde locks dyed for the role of Scully).

V. Christy and Blaine both seem to be representations of what the die-hard fans are like, with Chrissy sitting in a darkened room typing away at the computer (you can see she is on the Internet) and Blaine being amazingly obsessed with UFOs and science-fiction and saying "I just want to be taken away to some place where I don't have to worry about finding a job."

(Note: none of these reference solutions are claimed to be irrefutable, but they seem more or less accurate.)

"Avatar"

A troubled Skinner is framed for murder and Scully and Mulder investigate, despite his wishes for them not to. The board of professional conduct rules they are not to investigate and Skinner begins to witness a woman he envisions in his dreams...

X The prostitute may not be as dead as Mulder and Scully think. Take a closer look at the corpse when they go back to re-examine it for the glowing substance - the eyes flicker!
Continuity

X Well, the Board of Professional Conduct must have really thought they would be getting rid of Skinner this time, as they'd already turned his office into their own (having taken away his desk and brought in a bigger table). Even the corridor outside their office was the same as the one outside Skinner's. Or was that just some set re-dressing...?
Continuity

X If it really was a succubus that Skinner was seeing, wasn't she a bit old and haggard for such a role? A succubus is supposed to be beautiful and attractive, due to its nature; to seduce young men. (Or maybe the succubus was older because Walter is older?)
Subject Matter

Recurring Actors: Morris Paynch, Tasha Simms, Malcolm Stewart, Janie Woods-Morris

Best Line: A short snip from an early scene is one of the few instances of humour in this dark tale:
(after entering the very plush residence of the Escort Agency's manager)
Scully: "Business must be booming."
Mulder: "I think you mean banging."

Scenes: You could be forgiven for thinking that this one was very confusing and mysterious, as a scene was finally cut from the episode (featured in the script) that involved a conversation between the Cigarette-Smoking Man and Skinner. The scene explains why Skinner was set-up and makes it more obvious to the viewer that the Cigarette-Smoking Man had more to do with the murders than you think. Although the return of the Grey-Haired Man, who warned Skinner in **"Piper Maru"** about investigating Melissa Scully's death, does add some continuity.

Title Explanation: The name refers to the succubus mentioned in the episode, "avatar" meaning the supreme incarnation of a figure.

"Quagmire"

S cully opens her door one weekend to a Mulder begging her to go with him to investigate some cases of "Big Blue", a sea-serpent, and its connection to some murders. As they investigate, more people come to sticky ends along with someone else close to Scully.

X Mulder chases the "beast" through the forest, and eventually kills it, finding that it is, in fact, an alligator. Didn't said 'gator move mighty fast? I don't think those very short legs could move the very big body very fast.

Subject Matter

X Despite the fact that at the end of the story Mulder and Scully believe that, for a change, there is a more earthly explanation to the case, that of the alligator being the devouring monster, wouldn't they have found it strange that the one alligator was eating a lot of humans at a very fast rate? (Of course, we know that the Big Blue was real, after the diabolical ending - and the episode was going so well - but still, wouldn't they have searched for more alligators?)

Recurring Actors: Timothy Webber

Best Line: The entire "Conversation on The Rock" is memorable, but there were many other good exchanges between our duo:

> Scully: "You know on the old mariners' maps the cartographers would designate uncharted territories by writing 'Here be monsters'."

Mulder: "I've got a map of New York City just like that!"

And:

> (the pair discuss the subject of lake monsters)
> Mulder: "Sounds like you know a little something about the subject."
> Scully: "I did as a kid, but then I grew up and became a scientist."

Scenes: Chris Carter and Co. really enjoy killing off family members don't they? First it's William Scully, then Melissa, and now Scully's dog. And as for her brothers, well they didn't even turn up when she was returned from her abduction!

Also, this episode gave birth to the "Conversation on The Rock" (after the pilot's "Conversation on The Bed" and **"Tooms"** "Conversation in The Car"), amazingly, the entire segment was written by Darin Morgan and not Kim Newton, who is listed as the episode's writer.

Title Explanation: Another hidden meaning, as quagmire means swamp-like ground or a problematic situation. It's probably both, with the problems the agents encounter and the fact that the lake is too big to find Big Blue.

"Wetwired"

Anew source tips Mulder off about a set of mass-murders in a small town. The only link between the deaths are large collections of television recordings, which Mulder and Scully watch to see if a cause can be found. When Scully notices a small link, while becoming intensely paranoid about Mulder's activities, Mulder finds a more chilling answer.

X The opening shot with Mulder meeting his new informant raises a few questions. The car sits in the alley, surrounded by high walls to the left and right, yet there is a reflection on the front window of Capitol Hill; the question is, where is this reflection originating from? It contradicts all the surroundings.
Continuity

X Mulder and Scully watch the tapes taken from Patnick's home, and we are first treated with a shot of Mulder watching what appears to be a video tape (the picture is fast-forwarding, and Mulder uses the remote to stop it), yet the tape in the machine isn't actually in the machine, and just rests in the slot. The picture was being fed from another source (which was just a creators' shortcut).
Continuity

X When Mulder climbs down from the telephone pole, he steps off before the bottom onto the hood of his car, which wasn't parked there when he climbed up. Who parked it there?
Continuity

X After Scully has extensively watched the tapes, her mounting paranoia growing, she calls Mulder, gives the "Where are you?" line and,

149

thinking that she is being bugged, quickly cuts off the connection. In the moody light we see that Scully has a small mole beneath her nose. Scully doesn't have a beauty mark, unlike Gillian Anderson, who does have a mark which is covered up by make-up for the role of Agent Scully.
Continuity

X When we see Mrs Scully at home in bed, I found more evidence that the Scully brothers do not exist - the pictures on the bedside table are only of her two daughters. (Again, no sons. Suspicious.)
Continuity

X Here's one that unfortunately undermines the entire series: if Mulder really is red/green colour blind, surely he would have had quite a bit of difficulty entering the FBI as it is a condition which undermines judgement? It's not a serious condition, but surely it becomes a problem when his description could disagree with another agents in a serious case? Of course, it was just a plot device in this amazingly intense episode that made sure Mulder wasn't affected by the television poisoning and gave us a laugh about his bad ties.
Plot Discrepancy

X I was going to include the following nit-pick: if the Lone Gunmen are not colour blind, wouldn't they have been brainwashed also when examining the sample videotape? The answer? Well, they are paranoid enough aren't they?

Recurring Actors: Linden Banks, Colin Cunningham

Best Line: "Where are you?" More evidence of Gillian Anderson's amazing acting abilities as she

150

acts like the possessive partner (you relationshippers can take that any way you want to).

Scenes: It has been said that X is beginning to be hated by some fans as the evil bad guy, but even if he is actually playing for the other side, and not help- ing Mulder, I think it was good to see Steven Williams back in an episode this season, especially after the very short scenes he had in **"Nisei"** and **"731"**.

Title Explanation: To be "wetwired" is to have electronic information stored in the brain, a term used (or created) by cyber-author William Gibson.

To be "wetwired" is to have electronic information stored in the brain...

"Talitha Cumi"

A bizarre incident at a Fast Food Restaurant seems to have a correlation with Mrs Mulder having a stroke, but not a correlation Mulder was expecting. A complex plot eventually leads to clues and characters which are linked all the way back to Season Two's "Colony" and "End Game", and have some connection with the "Consortium" revealed to the viewer in "The Blessing Way", "Paper Clip", and "Apocrypha".

X Are we to believe that Mulder and Scully just stumbled upon the scene at the Fast Food Restaurant? A scene which would just happen to lead them to the cliff-hanger at the end? Yeah, right...
Plot Discrepancy

X If the Cigarette-Smoking Man really was an old friend of the Mulder family, wouldn't Mulder remember his name, or who he was? Previously in the series, Mulder has acted as he had never met the "Cancer Man", who even mentions that Mulder and Samantha were "young and energetic".
Continuity

X No one had been at the house in Quonochautaug (or however you spell and say it) for some time according to Mulder. Well someone must have, painting the house, as the paint on the door to the outside is wet - it even rubs off on Mulder's shoulder when he goes there and encounters X. (The Cigarette-Smoking Man must have been bored while waiting for Mrs Mulder to turn up.)
Continuity

X   They're obviously keen to stick with the new entrance to the FBI as we saw in "Pusher" as it's again different to the one seen in "The Blessing Way".
Continuity

> X   We're led to believe that "the weapon"/ice-pick-thingy is the only thing that can kill these shape-shifters, yet in **"Colony"** the fake Samantha tells Skinner and Mulder that a simple bullet at the back of the neck would be sufficient, the total opposite of X's words: "A simple bullet won't do." (Although after the problem the ice-pick causes in **"Herrenvolk"** - Season Four's opening episode, not listed in this volume - it's a good bet that no one knows exactly what will kill these beings.)
> **Continuity**

X   Didn't it take a bit long for someone to check out Jeremiah Smith and find that there were a group of men of the same name who were all identical, and registered civilians of the country? I know he didn't commit a crime, but the FBI and the police department did want to speak with him about what actually happened.
Plot Discrepancy

X   Sticking with the Jeremiah Smiths, they're not as clever as their predecessors, the Gregor-clones, are they? In **"Colony"** we learnt that the Gregors took different names, while all working at abortion clinics, yet here, all the men who look like Jeremiah Smith, have the name Jeremiah Smith. My, how inconspicuous. (Sometimes I wonder how many alien conspiracies there really are in the X-Files Universe.)
Continuity

✖ How did the "real" Jeremiah Smith know Scully was looking for him? Or even where she lived? He said himself that they had never met.

Plot Discrepancy

✖ And speaking of knowing where people are, how did the Bounty Hunter know where to find the trio at the end?

Recurring Actors: Stephen Dimopoulos, Bonnie Hay, Hrothgar Matthews, Angelo Vacco

Best Line: "You wanna smoke on that, or do you wanna smoke on this?"- Mulder to the Cigarette-Smoking Man while holding a gun in his face. Cockily enough, the Cigarette-Smoking Man says "Are you giving me a choice?"

Title Explanation: Taken from a passage in the Bible where Jesus commands a little girl to rise from the dead, Talitha Cumi means "little girl, arise". (Nit-pick alert! - there are no little girls rising in this episode!) The correlation with the episode itself is that Jeremiah Smith is capable of raising people from the dead with his healing powers. Also, we see Smith morph into the now very dead characters of Deep Throat and Bill Mulder (although they say no one dies on The X-Files, but we have seen their ghosts), so maybe they are also the living dead.

SEASON THREE
"FAMILY SCORECARD"

DANA SCULLY: The MJ Document trilogy continued with the loss of Melissa Scully - shot after being mistaken for Dana by Luis Cardinal. Dana gladly avenged Missy's death, the Scully-brothers remained absent (the question is - do they really exist?) and Margaret Scully survived, showing her negotiation skills (she would have been able to talk that gun away from Duane Barry if you ask me) when Dana became brainwashed by bizarre TV signals. Finally, Scully lost her dog... typical.

FOX MULDER: With Mrs Mulder being the only remaining member of the family apart from Fox, you had to wonder what could happen to her. She reveals at the beginning of the season that William Mulder "chose" Samantha to be taken away over Fox. And, she promptly suffers from a stroke at the end of the season after meeting the Cigarette-Smoking Man. The final question is; did they have an affair way-back-when? (Sick mental image! Sick, sick mental image!!)

Scully lost her dog... typical.

NUMBER CRUNCHING

Numbers usually play a part in an X-Files story, be it in a date, time, or file number. They are usually just randomly picked by the writer, or by the production team, usually inserted to give the sense of time passing or an event occurring. There are two numbers, that are, however, not so random. 1013 and 1121.

Chosen by Chris Carter, these numbers signify his wife's and his own birth dates, these being November 21st and October 13th respectively. Any chance there is that these dates appear, they will: most notably in the episodes he has written.

OCCURRENCES OF 1121
(DORI PIERSON'S - CHRIS CARTER'S WIFE - BIRTH DATE)

1X79: "Pilot"
- the time on Scully's clock: 11:21

1X01: "Deep Throat"
- Colonel Budahaus' birthday: 11/21/48

1X11: "Fire"
- X-file number, spoken by Scully at the end: 11214893

1X17: "Miracle Man"
- Time of autopsy: 11:21

1X23: "The Erlenmeyer Flask"
- the time on Scully's clock: 11:21

2X02: "The Host"	• the autopsy case: #DP112148 (initials and full birthday)
2X06: "Ascension"	• Mulder hears Scully's message on his answer-phone at 11:23, are we to assume she was abducted at 11:21?
2X13: "Irresistible"	• the time on Scully's clock: 11:21
2X16: "Colony"	• the time on Scully's motel room clock: 11:21
2X22: "F. Emasculata"	• the package containing the contaminated tissue: #DPP112148
3X02: "Paper Clip"	• Samantha Mulder's birthday: 11/21/65
3X15: "Piper Maru"	• seen as flight #1121 to Washington
3X24: "Talitha Cumi"	• the time when Mulder first visits his mother at the hospital: 11:21
3X24: "Talitha Cumi"	• the time when Scully is working at her computer: 11:21

OCCURRENCES OF 1013
(CHRIS CARTER'S BIRTH DATE)

Chris Carter's production company name - Ten Thirteen

1X01: "Deep Throat"
- case file #DF101364

2X02: "The Host"
- John Doe's catalogue number: 101356

2X17: "End Game"
- seen at the top of Mulder's e-mail: "To: Dana Scully, 001013"

3X02: "Paper Clip"
- Fox Mulder's birthday: 10/13/61

3X06: "2Shy"
- used as the time when Mulder and Scully get the results of the skin test: 10:13

3X10: "731"
- incorporated in the combination used to unlock the train door: #101331

3X16: "Apocrypha"
- the number on the door to the silo where Krycek is eventually trapped: 1013

THE BATH FILES

If you ever find yourself being investigated by Mulder and Scully, you should never consider going into the bathroom. Why? Because something bad happens, every time...

"Squeeze"
- Scully is attacked by Tooms, in the very first bathroom incident.

"Shadows"
- Lauren Kyte has a vision of Robert Graves' "suicide" when she goes into the bathroom.

"Ghost in the Machine"
- The company chairman is electrocuted when he answers the phone... in the bathroom (didn't figure that one out myself).

"Eve"
- Nothing actually happens in the bathroom, but while Mulder and Scully are in there, one of the young Eves puts digitalis in the drinks Mulder and Scully ordered.

"Shapes"
- While inside, Lyle turns into a werewolf.

"Host"
- A victim of the mutant flukeman coughs up a fluke-worm while taking a shower.

"Excelsius Dei"
- Mulder and a nurse are locked in a bathroom which is rapidly being filled with water.

"Die Hand Die Verletzt"
- The PTA-from-Hell plan to have Mulder and Scully killed in the school shower.

"Clyde Bruckman's Final Repose"

- Det. Havez is killed while leaving the bathroom. (I think it counts.)

"2Shy"

- Scully meets 2Shy on not-so-civil terms when she runs to the bath room to find supplies and save Ellen.

"731"

- Mulder discovers Ishimaru dead. Yes, he was killed in the toilet - garrotted by the Red-Haired Man (who actually doesn't have red hair).

"Revelations"

- Kevin is abducted from the bath room, after Scully has drawn his bath, and left him alone. (Will she ever learn...?)

"War of the Coprophages"

- One of the doctors at the hospital dies from a burst aneurysm when in the bathroom.

"Syzygy"

- After meeting Margi and Teri in the bathroom, a fellow Cheerleader is killed.

"Piper Maru"

- Krycek becomes possessed by the "oilien".

"Avatar"

- Scully comes into contact with some more not-so-friendly Men In Black.

THE X-FILES' DEATH TOLL

Apart from the supporting semi-regular cast, there are very few actors who can claim that they appeared on an episodes of The X-Files and survived. You see, most of the episodes of our beloved show involve Mulder and Scully investigating a string of mysterious murders (and they say the show isn't formulaic...), the press releases usually reading, "AGENTS MULDER AND SCULLY TRAVEL TO A SMALL TOWN TO INVESTIGATE A SET OF MYSTERIOUS MURDERS..."

Ever wondered how many have died in each episode? Here's the score:

[All deaths recorded have occurred *during* the episode, deaths that occur before are not included.]

SEASON ONE

1X79: "Pilot" 2
1X01: "Deep Throat" 0
1X02: "Squeeze" 2
1X03: "Conduit" 1
1X04: "The Jersey Devil" 1
1X05: "Shadows" 4
1X06: "Ghost in the Machine".2
       (unless you count the COS also "dying", which makes the
       total 3)
1X07: "Ice" 7
1X08: "Space" 1
1X09: "Fallen Angel" 9
1X10: "Eve" 3
1X11: "Fire" 1
1X12: "Beyond the Sea" 3
1X13: "Gender Bender" 6
1X14: "Lazarus" 3
1X15: "Young at Heart" 2
1X16: "EBE"   0
       (unless you count the EBE dying, which makes the total 1)
1X17: "Miracle Man"..........5
       (if Samuel Hartley really did "walk out", then it's only 4)
1X18: "Shapes" 3
1X19: "Darkness Falls" 31
1X20: "Tooms" 2
1X21: "Born Again" 2
1X22: "Roland" 2
1X23: "The Erlenmeyer Flask".4

SEASON ONE DEATH TOLL: ..96

SEASON TWO

2X01: "Little Green Men" 1
2X02: "The Host" 1
2X03: "Blood" 7
2X04: "Sleepless" 3
2X05: "Duane Barry" 0
2X06: "Ascension" 2
2X07: "Three" 6
2X08: "One Breath" 1
2X09: "Firewalker" 4
2X10: "Red Museum" 5
2X11: "Excelsius Dei" 2
2X12: "Aubrey" 2
2X13: "Irresistible" 1
2X14: "Die Hands Die Verletzt"6
2X15: "Fresh Bones" 2
2X16: "Colony" 7
2X17: "End Game"............6
       (minimum; don't forget the submarine's entire crew)
2X18: "Fearful Symmetry".....4
       (and that includes the elephant and the tiger)
2X19: "Dod Kalm" 4
2X20: "Humbug" 3
2X21: "The Calusari" 3
2X22: "F. Emasculata"........14
       (minimum; may have been more deaths in the prison)
2X23: "Soft Light" 7
2X24: "Our Town" 3
2X25: "Anasazi" 1

SEASON TWO DEATH TOLL: ..   95 (MINIMUM)

SEASON THREE

3X01: "The Blessing Way" 0
3X02: "Paper Clip" 2
3X03: "DPO" 2
3X04: "Clyde Bruckman's Final Repose"
........................6
3X05: "The List" 7
3X06: "2shy" 4
3X07: "The Walk" 5
3X08: "Oubliette" 1
3X09: "Nisei" 7
3X10: "731"..................3
(minimum; the hybrids at the facility were also killed)
3X11: "Revelations" 3
3X12: "War of the Coprophages" 5
3X13: "Syzygy" 5
3X14: "Grotesque" 3
3X15: "Piper Maru" 0
3X16: "Apocrypha" 1
3X17: "Pusher" 4
3X18: "Teso dos Bichos"......4
3X19: "Hell Money" 4
3X20: "Jose Chung's 'From Outer Space'"
........................0
3X21: "Avatar" 3
3X22: "Quagmire" 5
3X23: "Wetwired" 3
3X24: "Talitha Cumi" 0

SEASON THREE DEATH TOLL:.....75 (MINIMUM)

TOTAL X-FILES DEATH TOLL:
266 (MINIMUM)

AVERAGE NUMBER OF DEATHS (PER
EPISODE): 3 (AND HALF OF A BODY)

RECURRING ACTOR LISTING

As mentioned in the Introduction, many supporting cast members are reused as different characters in various episodes of The X-Files. So, each episode entry has a Recurring Actor section that has a list of names in. Each name can be cross referenced with the following list, and tells you which episodes the actor appeared in, as different characters.

The names are in alphabetical order, with each name being followed by the episode name with the character they portrayed in

A

Abrahams, Doug:

1X79: "Pilot" (Patrolman)
1X13: "Genderbender" (Agent #2)
2X14: "Die Hand Die Verletzt" (Paul Vitaris)
3X19: "Hell Money" (Lt. Neary)

A

Allford, Roger:

2X07: "3" (Garrett Lore)
3X09: "Nisei" (Harbourmaster)

A

Andersons, Mar:

2X19: "Dod Kalm" (Halverson)
3X03: "D.P.O." (Jack Hammond)

A

Angus, Forbes:

2X23: "Soft Light" (Govt. Scientist)
3X01: "The Blessing Way" (MD)

B

Bacic, Steve:

2X23: "Soft Light" (2nd Officer)
3X17: "Pusher" (Agent Collins)

B

Bain-Woodward, Meredith:

2X06: "Ascension" (Dr Ruth Slaughter)
3X17: "Pusher" (Defense Attorney)

B

Banks, Linden:

2X16: "Colony" (The Reverend Sistrunk)
3X23: "Wetwired" (Joseph Patnik)

B

Barber, Gillian:

1X06: "Ghost in the Machine"
(Agent Nancy Spiller)
2X10: "Red Museum" (Beth Kane)
3X09: "Nisei" (Penny)

B

Batten, Paul:

1X13: "Genderbender" (Brother Wilson)
3X15: "Piper Maru" (Dr Seizer)

B

Bauer, Marc:

1X06: "Ghost in the Machine" (Man in Suit)
2X02: "The Host" (Agent Brisentine)

B

Beley, Lisa Ann:

1X17: "Miracle Man" (Beatrice Salinger)
2X01: "Little Green Men" (Student)

B

Bivens, J.B.:

1X79: "Pilot" (Truck Driver)
2X17: "End Game" (Sharpshooter)

B

Boyd, Lynda:

1X11: "Fire" (Bar Patron)
2X22: "F. Emasculata" (Elizabeth)

B

Brazeau, Jay:

1X14: "Lazarus" (Prof. Varnes)
2X08: "One Breath" (Dr Daly)

B

Brunanski, Craig:

2X23: "Soft Light" (Security Guard)
3X05: "The List" (Guard)

B

Butler, Tom:

1X06: "Ghost in the Machine"
(Benjamin Drake)

2X16: "Colony" (Agent Ambrose Chapel)

C

Cecere, Fulvio:

2X01: "Little Green Men" (Aide)

3X11: "Revelations" (Priest)

C

Clothier, Robert:

2X10: "Red Museum" (Old Man)

3X15: "Piper Maru" (Chris Johansen)

C

Crane, Chilton:

1X17: "Miracle Man" (Margaret Hohman)

2X22: "F. Emasculata" (Mother at Bus
Station)

D

Davies, Glynis:

1X20: "Tooms" (Nelson)

2X13: "Irresistible" (Ellen)

3X06: "2Shy" (Monica)

3X23: "Wetwired" (Dr Stroman)

D

Diakun, Alex:

2X20: "Humbug" (Curator)

3X04: "Clyde Bruckman's Final Repose"
(Tarot Dealer)

3X20: "Jose Chung's 'From Outer Space'"
(Dr. Fingers)

D

Dimopoulos, Stephen:

2X19: "Dod Kalm" (Ionesco)

3X24: "Talitha Cumi" (Detective)

D

Dixon, Tim:

2X05: "Duane Barry" (Bob)

3X13: "Syzygy" (Dr Richard Godfrey)

D

Dobson, Michael:

2X05: "Duane Barry" (Marksman #2)

3X20: "Jose Chung's 'From Outer Space'"
(Lt. Schaeffer)

D

Dow, Bill:

1X04: "The Jersey Devil" (Dad)

2X21: "The Calusari" (Dr Charles Burk)

3X12: "War of the Coprophages" (Dr Newton)

D

Duborg, Kathleen:

2X03: "Blood" (Mother)

2X13: "Irresistible" (Prostitute)

E

Evans, Martin:

3X02: "Paper Clip" (Factotum)

3X16: "Apocrypha" (Majordomo)

E

Ewen, Lesley:

1X79: "Pilot" (Receptionist)
1X13: "Genderbender" (Agent #1)
3X11: "Revelations" (Carina Maywald)

F

Frazier, Guyle:

2X07: "3" (Officer)
2X23: "Soft Light" (Barney)

F

Fredericks, David:

2X03: "Blood" (Security Guard)
3X08: "Oubliette" (Mr Larken)

G

Gale, Lorena:

1X05: "Shadows" (Ellen Bledsoe)
2X08: "One Breath" (Nurse Wilkins)

H

Hayes, Deryl:

1X05: "Shadows" (Webster)
2X01: "Little Green Men" (Agent Morris)
3X07: "The Walk" (Army Doctor)

H

Heaton, Tom:

1X05: "Shadows" (Groundskeeper)
3X12: "War of the Coprophages" (Resident #1)

H

Henderson, Fred:

1X12: "Beyond the Sea" (Agent Thomas)
2X05: "Duane Barry" (Agent Rich)

H

Herrera, Maria:

1X10: "Eve" (Guard #2)
3X12: "War of the Coprophages" (Customer #1)

H

Hetherington, Gary:

1X02: "Squeeze" (Kennedy)
2X01: "Little Green Men" (Lewin)

H

Humphreys, Alf:

1X08: "Space" (2nd Controller)
3X01: "The Blessing Way" (Dr Pomerantz)

J

Johnson, P. Lynn:

1X21: "Born Again" (Dr Sheila Braun)
2X14: "Die Hand Die Verletzt"
        (Deborah Brown)

J

Johnston, Andrew:

1X01: "Deep Throat" (Colonel Budahas)
2X16: "Colony" (Agent Weiss)
2X17: "End Game" (Agent Weiss)

K

Kaye, David:

2X09: "Firewalker" (Eric Parker)
3X16: "Apocrypha" (Doctor)

K

Kelamis, Peter:

1X14: "Lazarus" (O'Dell)
2X15: "Fresh Bones" (Lt. Foyle)

K

Kosterman, Mitchell:

1X13: "Genderbender",
2X04: "Sleepless" (Det. Horton)
3X05: "The List" (Fornier)

K

Kramer, Ken:

1X23: "The Erlenmeyer Flask" (Dr Berube)
2X07: "3" (Dr Browning)
3X12: "War of the Coprophages" (Dr Ivanov)

L

LaCroix, Peter:

1X16: "E.B.E." (Ranheim/Frank Druce)
2X06: "Ascension" (Dwight)

L

Lane, Campbell:

1X17: "Miracle Man" (Margaret's Father)
2X21: "The Calusari" (Calusari #3)

L

Lea, Nicholas:

1X13: "Genderbender" (Michael)
2X04: "Sleepless"
2X05   "Duane Barry"
2X06: "Ascension"
2X25: "Anasazi"
3X01: "The Blessing Way"
3X02: "Paper Clip"
3X15: "Piper Maru"
3X16: "Apocrypha" (Agent Alex Krycek)

L

Lewis, David:

1X04: "The Jersey Devil" (Young Officer)
2X09: "Firewalker" (Vosberg)
3X08: "Oubliette" (Young Agent)

L

Lewis, Robert:

1X10: "Eve" (Officer)
2X05: "Duane Barry" (Officer)
3X02: "Paper Clip" (ER Doctor)

L

Lysell, Allan:

1X16: "E.B.E." (Chief Rivers)
2X17: "End Game" (Able Gardner)

M

MacDonald, William:

1X09: "Fallen Angel" (Dr Oppenheim)
2X02: "The Host" (Federal Marshal)
3X06: "2Shy" (Agent Kazanjian)

M

MacKay, Don:

1X12: "Beyond the Sea" (Warden Joseph Cash)
2X02: "The Host" (Charlie)
3X17: "Pusher" (Judge)

M

Makaj, Steve:

2X06: "Ascension" (Patrolman)
3X03: "D.P.O." (Frank Kiveat)

M

Mathew, Sue:

1X22: "Roland" (Lisa Dole)
3X16: "Apocrypha" (Agent Caleca)

M

Matthews, Hrothgar:

1X04: "The Jersey Devil" (Jack)
2X02: "The Host" (Man on Phone)
2X24: "Our Town" (Mental Patient)
3X24: "Talitha Cumi" (Galen)

M

McBeath, Tom:

1X08: "Space" (Scientist)
2X07: "3" (Det. Munson)
3X18: "Teso Dos Bichos" (Dr Lewton)

M

McFee, Dwight:

1X18: "Shapes" (David Gates)
2X01: "Little Green Men" (Commander)
2X13: "Irresistible" (Suspect)
3X04: "Clyde Bruckman's Final Repose"
(Detective Havez)

M

McKay, David:

2X05: "Duane Barry" (FBI Agent)
3X04: "Clyde   Bruckman's   Final   Repose"
(Mr Gordon)

M

McLean, Paul:

1X18: "Shapes" (Dr Josephs)
2X25: "Anasazi" (Agent Kautz)
3X09: "Nisei" (Coast Guard Officer)

M

McNulty, Kevin:

1X02: "Squeeze" & 3X16:"Apocrypha" (Fuller)
2X23: "Soft Light" (Dr Davey)

M

Miller, Gabrielle:

2X24: "Our Town" (Paula Gray)
3X13: "Syzygy" (Brenda J. Summerfield)

M

Miller, Stephen E.:
1X79: "Pilot" (Truitt)
2X05: "Duane Barry" (Tactical Commander)

M

Morriseau, Renae:
1X18: "Shapes" (Gwen Goodensnake)
2X25: "Anasazi" (Josephine Doane)

P

Payne, John:

1X23: "The Erlenmeyer Flask" (Guard)
2X20: "Humbug" (Glazebrook)

P

Puttonen, Michael:

1X01: "Deep Throat" (Motel Manager)
2X04: "Sleepless" (Dr Pilsson)
3X10: "731" (Conductor)

R

Reid, Rick:

1X79: "Pilot" (Astronomer)
2X21: "The Calusari" (Steve Holvey)

R

Rennie, Callum Keith:

1X14: "Lazarus" (Tommy)
2X15: "Fresh Bones" (Groundskeeper)

R

Roberts, Ken:

2X16: "Colony" (Proprietor)

3X04: "Clyde Bruckman's Final Repose"
(Clerk)

R

Robertson, Alan:

1X11: "Fire" (Gray-Haired Man)

3X18: "Teso Dos Bichos" (Roosevelt)

R

Rogers, Michael:

1X09: "Fallen Angel" (Lt. Griffin)

2X16: "Colony" (1st Crewman)

R

Rose, Gabrielle:

1X01: "Deep Throat" (Anita Budahas)

2X02: "The Host" (Dr Zenzola)

S

Sanders, Alvin:

1X09: "Fallen Angel" (Deputy Wright)
2X22: "F. Emasculata" (Bus Driver)

S

Sandomirsky, Kerry:

1X22: "Roland" (Tracy)
3X06: "2Shy" (Joanne Steffen)

S

Saunders, Mark:

1X14: "Lazarus" (Doctor #2)
2X13: "Irresistible" (Agent Busch)

S

Sauve, Ron:

2X02: "The Host" (Foreman)
3X18: "Teso Dos Bichos" (Mr Decker)

S

Simms, Tasha:

1X10: "Eve" (Ellen Reardon)
2X11: "Excelsis Dei" (Laura Kelly)
3X21: "Avatar" (Jay Cassal)

S

Sparks, Carrie Cain:

2X24: "Our Town" (Maid)
3X09: "Nisei" (Train Station Clerk)

S

Stewart, Bobby L.:

2X06: "Ascension" (Deputy)
3X12: "War of the Coprophages" (Resident #2)

S

Stewart, Malcolm:

1X79: "Pilot" (Dr Glass)
2X07: "3" (Commander Carver)
3X21: "Avatar" (Agent Bonnecaze)

T

Thompson, Don:

1X03: "Conduit" (Holtzman)
2X04: "Sleepless" (Henry Willig)
3X07: "The Walk" (Lt. Col. Victor Stans)

T

Tipple, Gordon:

1X10: "Eve" (Detective)
1X15: "Young at Heart" (Joe Crandall)
2X20: "Humbug" (Hepcat Helm)

T

Touliatos, George:

1X10: "Eve" (Dr Katz)
2X03: "Blood" (Larry Winter)

T

Turner, Frank C.:

1X20: "Tooms" (Dr Collins)
2X05: "Duane Barry" (Dr Hakkie)

T

Twa, Kate:

1X13: "Genderbender" (female Marty)

2X23: "Soft Light" (Det. Ryan)

V

Vacco, Angelo:

2X22: "F. Emasculata" (Angelo Garza)

3X24: "Talitha Cumi" (Doorman)

W

Webber, Timothy:

1X20: "Tooms" (Det. Talbot)

2X24: "Our Town" (Jess Harold)

3X22: "Quagmire" (Dr Farraday)

W

Wilde, Bob:

2X01: "Little Green Men" (Rand)

3X09: "Nisei" (Limousine Driver)

Now in a galaxy not far from you...

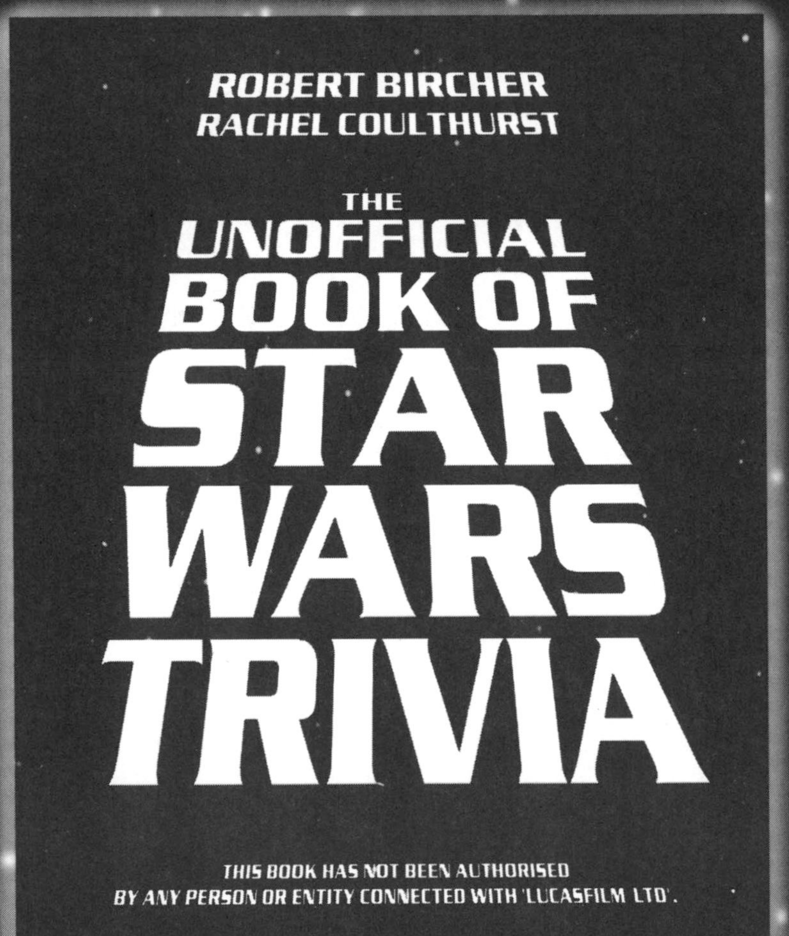

Summersdale